PKSOI PAPER

LESSONS LEARNED FROM U.S. GOVERNMENT LAW ENFORCEMENT IN INTERNATIONAL OPERATIONS

Dilshika Jayamaha
Scott Brady
Ben Fitzgerald
Jason Fritz

December 2010

*****

Comments pertaining to this report are invited and should be forwarded to: Director, Strategic Studies Institute, U.S. Army War College, 122 Forbes Ave, Carlisle, PA 17013-5244.

*****

All Strategic Studies Institute (SSI) publications are available on the SSI homepage for electronic dissemination. Hard copies of this report also may be ordered from our homepage. SSI's homepage address is: *www.StrategicStudiesInstitute.army.mil*.

The website address for the Peacekeeping and Stability Operations Institute (PKSOI) is *https://pksoi.army.mil*.

*****

The Strategic Studies Institute publishes a monthly e-mail newsletter to update the national security community on the research of our analysts, recent and forthcoming publications, and upcoming conferences sponsored by the Institute. Each newsletter also provides a strategic commentary by one of our research analysts. If you are interested in receiving this newsletter, please subscribe on our homepage at *www.StrategicStudiesInstitute.army.mil/newsletter/*.

ISBN 1-58487-470-8

CONTENTS

FOREWORD

The role of law enforcement is becoming increasingly prominent in the conduct of international operations involving the U.S. Government (USG), including counterinsurgency, peace operations, and reconstruction and stabilization. Hence, it is important for practitioners (military and civilian) and policymakers to understand how law enforcement can contribute to the achievement of U.S. strategic objectives and how it integrates into a wider interagency mission structure. This Peacekeeping and Stability Operations Institute (PKSOI) Paper should add to the body of knowledge in this field by presenting the findings from an analysis of U.S. law enforcement contributions to three major post-Cold War commitments.

This report is the product of a year of research conducted by Noetic, under contract by the Emerging Capabilities Division Ground Portfolio Director, Colonel Patrick N. Kelleher, U.S. Marine Corps, within the Rapid Reaction Technology Office of the Office of the Secretary of Defense. This was part of the Law Enforcement Capabilities Project (LECP) which aims to inform USG agencies about issues relevant to law enforcement capabilities on international operations. The Institute for Defense Analyses (IDA) also contributed to the project, with Mr. William Simpkins playing a key role in the research phase. The project team particularly acknowledges the United States Marshals Service (USMS) and the Department of Justice's International Criminal Investigative Training Assistance Program (ICITAP), whose support was invaluable in facilitating research visits to Colombia and Kosovo, respectively. The team also received research and liaison support from representatives of: the Department of State, the Department of Defense, the Department of Justice, the Department of Homeland Security, the United States Agency for International Development, and the United States Army. Input obtained from these representatives has been critical in the preparation of this document; however, the views expressed here are Noetic's, are not official government statements, and are not the official views of the USG. Any errors in this paper are the responsibility of the authors and not any representative of the USG.

The approach taken by the project team and the access facilitated by the interagency participants have permitted a unique and detailed analysis of the subject matter based on recent USG experience. The lessons learned are invaluable for informing future USG endeavors to integrate the full range of law enforcement capabilities, authorities, and perspectives into international operations to achieve national objectives.

DOUGLAS C. LOVELACE, JR.
Director
Strategic Studies Institute

STEPHEN T. SMITH
Colonel, U.S. Army
Director
Peacekeeping and Stability
Operations Institute

SUMMARY

Law enforcement (LE) personnel, agencies, techniques, equipment and priorities have been an increasingly prominent feature within U.S. Government (USG) commitments to international operations.[1] This is a reflection of the increased human and societal complexity of the operational environments in which the USG has intervened and the multifaceted nature of the objectives often sought by the USG in these international operations.

The most obvious manifestation of LE on international operations is the presence of American police officers working as a part of uniformed international police missions (U.S.-led, coalition, or multinational). However, these interim policing missions are only part of the contribution to international operations that can be made by LE. U.S. LE agencies may also be involved directly in international operations as a part of their standing authorities related to the enforcement of U.S. domestic law; contribute LE expertise in capacity building and institutional reform efforts; or as support and assistance to U.S. military forces employed in LE-related roles and in the conduct of their military tasks.

Given the complexity of USG LE involvement in contemporary international operations, it is important to understand how these agencies work, what roles they play, or could play, in the conduct of operations, and how their various initiatives relate to one another. As such, this analysis specifically examines lessons from four relevant aspects of LE involvement in international operations, recognizing that observations that are discussed in this paper do not constitute the entirety of lessons from each of the operations. These aspects include three operational case studies from USG post-Cold War experience in international operations: Panama (1989-99), Colombia (1989-Present), and Kosovo (1998-Present). These three operations were selected because they provided examples across a wide spectrum of U.S. involvement and have either already been completed or are nearing completion—allowing for analysis of their results as mature operations. Additionally, this analysis included an investigation of technological capabilities used by the military and law enforcement organizations that undergird the provision of LE and military capabilities in international operational environments in order to analyze capability gaps and points of technological synchronization between the two communities.[2]

LAW ENFORCEMENT CAPABILITIES PROJECT

This paper has been produced as a part of the Law Enforcement Capabilities Project (LECP). The LECP is an initiative of the Emerging Capabilities Division (ECD) within the Rapid Reaction Technology Office (RRTO) of the Office of the Secretary of Defense (OSD). The RRTO has funded this project in order to help inform policy and capability development decisions related to the contributions and integration of USG agencies and bureaus with law enforcement responsibilities and expertise, and the employment of U.S. military elements in law enforcement-related or supporting roles in international operations.

This paper will be used to inform further research and concept development and is being published independently to contribute to the advancement of thinking in this area. The second phase of the LECP will consist of a series of exercises, each examining a component of USG law enforcement in international operations: LE support to the U.S. military, interim expeditionary LE, and host nation LE capacity building and institutional reform. These exercises will be followed by an exercise that will examine the total problem space of U.S. LE in international operations.

METHODOLOGY

This paper presents the results of the analysis conducted in relation to the case studies of USG LE involvement in international operations. For each element (three operations and the technology section), the analysis was based on unclassified information and was conducted in three stages:

- **Desk research.** Baseline desk research relying heavily on advice, support, and access to information made possible by engagement with representatives from numerous USG agencies.
- **Primary source research.** Included extensive outreach to subject matter experts (SMEs), practitioners, and policymakers within USG agencies who participated in the three operations or with involvement in employment of relevant military and LE technologies. For Kosovo and Colombia, the primary research was augmented by in-country field research.
- **Lessons learned workshops.** The observations and lessons developed through desk research and primary source research were subjected to structured examination and discussion in a series of workshops with SMEs. The workshops served two purposes: to share and validate observations, and to develop recommendations.

CASE STUDIES

This paper will consider three case studies.

Panama.

Coming right after the fall of the Berlin Wall, Panama is considered the first "post Cold War" USG military intervention. Though launched primarily to oust Manuel Noriega from power and bring him to trial in the United States (Operation JUST CAUSE), the operation quickly became an institution-building exercise, with the United States both providing LE capabilities and rebuilding Panamanian law enforcement institutions over several years (Operation PROMOTE LIBERTY and subsequent USG operations). The effort in Panama was executed primarily by the Department of Defense (DoD) in the form of military units, the U.S. Marshals Service (USMS), the International Criminal Investigations Training Assistance Program (ICITAP), the Drug Enforcement Administration (DEA), and the Department of State (DoS). The analysis of operations in Panama was conducted along three lines of operation (LOO):

- Law enforcement-related LOOs for Operation JUST CAUSE, including the Noriega extradition, exercising detainee warrants, passenger screening, and airport security;
- Operation PROMOTE LIBERTY and the transition phase, including the maintenance of law and order and the reestablishment of host nation law enforcement capacity; and,

- Civilian-led reconstruction and stabilization, focused on building host nation civilian law enforcement capabilities.

Colombia.

USG LE work in Colombia stemmed from efforts to stop the flow of narcotics into the United States. The Andean Counter Drug Initiative, a counternarcotics plan devised in the late 1980s, extended USG LE and other counternarcotics assistance to Peru, Bolivia, and Colombia. Over almost 2 decades, U.S. support to Colombia, in particular, has shifted into a comprehensive government-to-government partnership to disrupt drug networks, including through the reform and improvement of domestic LE capabilities. Plan Colombia and subsequent and parallel efforts have required cooperation across USG departments and agencies to help Colombia build military, paramilitary, and civilian LE institutions. The major agencies engaged in Colombia were the U.S. Agency for International Development (USAID); the DoS (Western Hemisphere Affairs, International Narcotics Affairs and Law Enforcement Affairs [INL]); the DoD; the Department of Justice (ICITAP); the Federal Bureau of Investigation (FBI); the DEA (U.S. Drug Enforcement Administration); the ATF (Bureau of Alcohol, Tobacco, Firearms, and Explosives); the Office of Overseas Prosecutorial Development Assistance and Training (OPDAT); the USMS; and the Department of the Treasury.

Analysis of these operations focused on three LOOs:

- Counternarcoterrorism operations, including aerial and manual eradication and interdiction operations; U.S.-led maritime, aerial, and riverine interdiction and support; border security;

the Judicial Wire Intercept (Wiretap) Program; and the use of extraterritorial laws to prosecute drug crimes;

- Law enforcement and rule of law training, including ICITAP general purpose training and specific training from the FBI, DEA, and USMS; and,
- Capacity and institution building focused on legal reforms and mentoring and advising host nation institutions.

Kosovo.

Unlike the other two operations, USG involvement in Kosovo had no direct linkage to U.S. law enforcement concerns. Rather, it is an example of the necessity of LE contributions as a part of a wider multinational operation in support of USG foreign policy objectives. It also required the need to establish security in the host nation as part of an international coalition while simultaneously building a new nation's LE institutions from scratch. The key USG players in Kosovo operations are the DoD; ICITAP and OPDAT; and the DoS (INL and the Bureau of European and Eurasian Affairs). These operations were analyzed in three LOOs:

- Deployed law enforcement operations; observers and advisers, focusing on the observer mission; interim law enforcement and monitoring, mentoring, and advising (MMA); and post-independence MMA and the continued executive mandate;
- Capacity-building of Kosovo ministries and agencies, divided into multilateral and bilateral programs; and,

- Military Kosovo Force (KFOR) operations, such as legal reform, mentoring and advising, and employment of general purpose forces.

Conclusions.

The analysis in this project shows the pervasive and complex role that law enforcement and related issues have played in U.S. involvement in contemporary international operations. The analysis also revealed some of the cross-cutting issues involved in the employment of technology on such operations involving both military and law enforcement agencies.[3] Despite the unique circumstances and history of each operation, there were key findings that are common to all operations considered:

- In all operations considered, the length of commitment of USG resources to deal with law enforcement issues has exceeded original planning estimates—often by many years.
- Capacity building in law enforcement has been a required and substantial element of all of these operations.
- Military forces played a key role in law enforcement and related issues, even if not specifically tasked with a law enforcement mandate.
- Much of the required expertise and authority for law enforcement operations and related capacity building/institutional reform currently exists in civilian agencies across the USG, but coordinating across the USG has been ad hoc with mixed results.

ENDNOTES - SUMMARY

1. "International operations" is used here as a term to describe the range of USG commitment of resources as an intervention in another nation in support of U.S. national objectives. It involves all commitments beyond the normal conduct of state-to-state diplomacy but beneath the threshold of conventional conflict. As such, this includes military operations other than war (including reconstruction and stabilization, counterinsurgency, peace support, and humanitarian assistance operations), as well as comprehensive support of a less predominantly military nature provided to another state.

2. The Technology Case Study is only available as a supplementary annex to the electronically-published version of this report, and is available from *pksoi.army.mil/*.

3. *Ibid.*

LESSONS LEARNED FROM U.S. GOVERNMENT LAW ENFORCEMENT IN INTERNATIONAL OPERATIONS

CHAPTER 1

INTRODUCTION

Law enforcement (LE) personnel, agencies, techniques, equipment, and priorities have been an increasingly prominent feature within the United States Government (USG) commitment to numerous international operations,[1] particularly since the end of the Cold War. This is a reflection of the increased human and societal, as opposed to military or geostrategic, complexity of the operational environments into which the USG has intervened and the multifaceted nature of the objectives often sought by the USG in these international operations. In recent decades, the use of military force alone has rarely been sufficient to achieving the desired end states sought by the USG. Often, there is a requirement to establish both security and stability as a part of the operation and to provide support to, expand the capacity of, or reestablish host nation authority to sustain this stability. LE is a critical element of security and is also a bridge toward building an effective Rule of Law (RoL) system that helps restore and maintain legitimate civil governance.

The most obvious manifestation of LE on international operations is the presence of American police officers working as a part of uniformed international police missions (USG-led, coalition, or multinational) that are used to maintain law and order in support of or in the absence of host nation authority. This has been seen in many recent operational environments.

However, these interim policing missions are only part of the contribution to international operations that can be made by LE. U.S. LE agencies may also be involved directly in international operations as a part of their standing authority related to the enforcement of U.S. domestic law; this is often conducted in conjunction with host nation and/or international police. Another contribution of LE expertise is in the capacity building and institutional reform efforts to enhance or rebuild a host nation's (HN) LE and related institutions that are necessary to sustain security and effective governance. Furthermore, U.S. military forces are increasingly employed in LE-related or supporting roles and simultaneously using LE assistance in the conduct of their military tasks in these environments.

Given the complexity of USG LE involvement in contemporary international operations, it is important to understand how these agencies work, what roles they play, or could play, in the conduct of operations, and how their various initiatives relate to one another. Such an understanding will help guide thinking about how to conduct and coordinate these efforts in future international operations.

Aim.

This paper presents the results of an examination of various applications of USG LE capabilities in several contexts and offers a series of observations and recommendations. The lessons analyzed in this paper are only those regarding strategic and operational levels; identification of tactical-level lessons was not in the scope of this project. This analysis is presented with the aim of informing decisions about policy and capability development and integration relating to the employment of LE capabilities/expertise and the use of military in LE-related roles and in supporting LE on international operations.

This report specifically examines lessons from three case studies of LE involvement in international operations, in particular USG post-Cold War experience in international operations.[2] The three case studies are:

- **Panama (1989-99).** Coming right after the fall of the Berlin Wall, Panama is considered the first "post Cold War" USG military intervention. Though launched primarily to oust Manuel Noriega from power and bring him to trial in the United States, the operation quickly became a state-building exercise, with the United States both providing LE capabilities and rebuilding Panamanian law enforcement institutions over several years. The effort in Panama reshaped the USG organizational landscape for such operations.
- **Colombia (1989-present).** USG LE work in Colombia began with efforts to stop the flow of narcotics into the United States. The Andean Counter Drug Initiative, a counternarcotics plan devised in the late 1980s, extended USG LE and other counternarcotics assistance to Peru, Bolivia, and Colombia. Over almost 2 decades, U.S. support to Colombia in particular, has shifted into a comprehensive government-to-government partnership to disrupt drug networks, including through the reform and improvement of domestic LE capabilities. Plan Colombia and subsequent efforts have required unparalleled cooperation across USG departments and agencies to help Colombia build

military, paramilitary, and civilian LE institutions.

- **Kosovo (1998-present).** Unlike the other two operations, USG involvement in Kosovo had no direct linkage to U.S. law enforcement concerns. Rather, it is an example of the necessity of LE contributions as a part of a wider multinational operation in support of USG foreign policy objectives. It also required the need to establish security in the host nation as part of an international coalition while simultaneously building a new nation's LE institutions from scratch.

Law Enforcement Capabilities Project.

This paper has been produced as a part of the Law Enforcement Capabilities Project (LECP). The LECP is an initiative of the Emerging Capabilities Division (ECD) within the Rapid Reaction Technology Office (RRTO) of the Office of the Secretary of Defense (OSD). The RRTO has funded this project to help inform policy and capability development decisions related to the contributions of USG agencies and bureaus with law enforcement responsibilities and expertise and the employment of U.S. military elements in LE related or supporting roles. It is also interested in the integration of various interagency (IA) initiatives as a part of international operations.

This paper will be used to inform further research and concept development and is being published independently for others to use in support of further developing LE capabilities.

Methodology.

The chapter presents the results of the analysis that was conducted in relation to the aforementioned case studies of USG LE involvement in international operations. For each case study, the analysis was conducted in three stages:

- **Desk research.** Baseline desk research provided the context of each operation, analysis of the policymaking processes surrounding each, data on strategic and operational implementation, and an existing set of lessons learned through available academic and practitioner literature. This phase of research relied heavily on advice, support, and access to information made possible by engagement with representatives from numerous USG agencies.
- **Primary source research.** This included extensive outreach to subject matter experts, practitioners, and policymakers within USG agencies who participated in the three operations or with involvement in employment of relevant military and LE technologies. The project team conducted 70 interviews in support of this research. In addition, many interviewees made additional primary source documentation available to the project team. All interviews and documentation for this analysis are unclassified. The U.S. Army Military Police Historian also made further information available. For Kosovo and Colombia, the primary research was augmented by in-country field research to study operational practice first-hand. This enabled further discussions and interviews with USG subject-matter experts (SMEs) and

practitioners in the field, as well as HN counterparts working on the relevant issues. The observations that were drawn through interviews and site visits were collated, and lessons were drawn out at the macro level for further discussion.

- **Lessons learned workshops.** Finally, the observations and lessons developed through desk research and primary source research were subjected to structured examination and discussion in a series of workshops with SMEs. In addition to Panama, Colombia and Kosovo, a functional workshop was held on technology to examine the employment of technology by LE personnel and military forces and their potential application in international operations.[3] A wide range of agencies and SMEs, practitioners, and individuals with experience in the various operations participated in the workshops. The workshops served two purposes:
  - **Share and validate observations.** Each of the strategic and operational level observations that were drawn through research, interviews, and site visits were shared with participants during the discussions for them to validate and provide additional insights.
  - **Develop recommendations.** The various SMEs from across the IA developed the recommendations documented herein in a structured workshop. The LECP team have undertaken additional analysis and structured the recommendations, but the base recommendations represent the unofficial views of SMEs with direct policy, leadership, or operational experience in the areas covered.

Interagency Participation.

This project would not have been possible without significant support from across the IA, think tanks, and individuals who have since retired from government service. The project team would like to recognize the support of the following organizations:

- **Department of State.** Office of the Coordinator for Reconstruction and Stabilization (S/CRS); Bureau of Political-Military Affairs; Bureau of International Narcotics and Law Enforcement Affairs (INL); Narcotics Affairs Section (NAS); Bureau of Western Hemisphere Affairs (Office of Andean Affairs, Office of Policy Planning and Coordination); and Bureau of European and Eurasian Affairs (Office of South Central European Affairs and Office of U.S. Assistance Coordinator for Europe and Eurasia).
- **Department of Justice.** International Criminal Investigative Training Assistance Program (ICITAP); Office of Overseas Prosecutorial Development, Assistance and Training (OPDAT); the Drug Enforcement Administration (DEA); the U.S. Marshals Service (USMS); and the Federal Bureau of Investigation (FBI).
- **Department of Defense.** Office of the Secretary of Defense-Policy (Special Operations/ Low-Intensity Conflict and Interdependent Capabilities [SO/LIC&IC]); Joint Staff; Headquarters Department of the Army, Office of the Provost Marshal General (OPMG); U.S. Army Military Police Corps School; U.S. Army Peacekeeping and Stability Operations Institute (PKSOI); United States Marine Corps, Center for

Irregular Warfare (USMC CIW); United States Southern Command (SOUTHCOM); Joint Interagency task Force South (JIATF-S); and the Institute for Defense Analyses (IDA).

- **Department of Homeland Security (DHS).** Office for State and Local Law Enforcement (OSLLE); United States Coast Guard (USCG); and Federal Emergency Management Agency (FEMA).
- **Department of the Treasury.** Office of Foreign Assets Control (OFAC).
- **United States Agency for International Development (USAID).**
- **Embassy of the United States of America in Bogota, Colombia.**
- **Embassy of the United States of America in Pristina, Kosovo.**

Qualifications and Limitations.

The observations that are discussed in this paper do not constitute the entirety of lessons from each of the operations. For purposes of focusing on LE and related topics, the observations contain only the primary themes observed through research and interviews. In addition, the background information is not intended to be a definitive history of each of the case studies. The information and descriptions are used to try to understand what happened in each of the operations rather than presenting a definitive narration of events.

In order to be able to account for and analyze each of the various strands of law enforcement initiatives conducted by the USG, this research has identified distinct Lines of Operation (LOO) for each operation. These LOOs were developed by the project team purely to guide research and to allow coherent consideration of the aims of separate initiatives and the role played by various agencies in contributing to each. It must be stressed that these LOOs were developed by the LECP project team for analytical purposes and do not reflect any contemporary planning approach used by the USG in the operations considered.

The project team encountered some important gaps in information in relation to the strategic and operational decisions taken by the agencies, especially in relation to Panama due to the time that has lapsed since the end of the operation. The analysis was also limited to the unclassified information domain, reducing the ability to examine classified records of senior policymaking (National Security Council decision memorandum, operations orders, etc.). These gaps have resulted in limitations in the level of detail that can be provided in some areas, but have not undermined the team's ability to analyze the fundamental areas of interest of the project.

ENDNOTES - CHAPTER 1

1. "International operations" is used here to describe the range of USG commitment of resources as an intervention in another nation in support of U.S. national objectives. It involves all commitments beyond the normal conduct of state-to-state diplomacy but beneath the threshold of conventional conflict. As such, this includes military operations other than war (including reconstruction and stabilization, counterinsurgency, peace support, and humanitarian assistance operations), as well as comprehensive support of a less predominantly military nature provided to another state.

2. The Law Enforcement Capabilities Project (LECP) also conducted a study examining issues related to the employment of technological capabilities that undergird the provision of LE

and military capabilities in international operational environments. This case study looks at technology needs of LE entities and military forces in population-centric operations, the potential for sharing of military and LE capabilities to support respective priorities, and differing approaches to the employment of technology between the military and law enforcement communities. The Technology Case Study is only available as a supplementary annex to the electronically-published version of this report, and is available from *www.pksoi.army.mil*.

3. *Ibid*.

CHAPTER 2

PANAMA

INTRODUCTION

In December 1989 when President George H. W. Bush directed U.S. military forces to "protect the lives of American citizens in Panama and to bring General Noriega to justice in the United States," he did not commit to rebuilding the Panamanian state from the ground up. He chose a goal that would be easily understood. He hinted at the tasks to come only by saying "the United States is eager to work with the Panamanian people in partnership and friendship to rebuild their economy."[1]

Yet within hours of the commencement of Operation JUST CAUSE (and before the military operation was complete), it was clear that the U.S. Government (USG) would need a broad interagency (IA) effort to enable and rebuild vital structures within the host nation, especially its law enforcement capabilities. The efforts that were started in 1989 would continue for 10 years. The security vacuum created by rapid military success had to be filled by the victors. The Panamanian police and the Rule of Law (RoL) system both had to be recreated, and these massive tasks stretched the USG entities in the country at the time. The U.S. military, which had the most resources and personnel in country, had to fill the void by providing interim security and limited amounts of law enforcement and capacity building through deployment of Military Police (MPs) and some civil affairs soldiers. The military had not, however, planned for such an effort and did not have the legal authority to build civilian law enforcement entities overseas.

Operations in Panama forced the United States to quickly adapt to the challenges of integrated civil-military post-combat reconstruction and stabilization operations. The U.S. military established new entities in the field, and civilian agencies took on new missions. The Department of Justice (DoJ) International Criminal Investigative Training Assistance Program (ICITAP) was tasked to rapidly change its mission and duties and begin reconstituting the Panamanian police—this unexpected change led to the ICITAP remaining in the country for the next 10 years to rebuild the police system and train personnel.

The Panama operation highlights challenges that the USG continues to face at the strategic and operational levels for any comprehensive effort to support law enforcement (LE) needs of international operations. The Panama example showed a certain level of adaptation among USG entities that were involved in the mission, but its lessons remain applicable today as IA coordination, military and civilian integration, and significant gaps in capacities and authorities continue to cause the United States great difficulties in these missions.

This section contains the following areas: (1) A synopsis of the Panama operation and LE Lines of Operation; (2) Observations drawn through research and interviews; and (3) Recommendations drawn through workshop discussion and analysis.

SYNOPSIS (1989-99)

Operation JUST CAUSE (OJC) was in planning for more than 2 years prior to actual U.S. intervention. OJC was launched after the failure of efforts to remove General Manuel Noriega from power following his indictment in the United States on drug trafficking charges and as his domestic popularity plummeted in the wake of allegations of stolen elections. Tensions increased with Noriega's consolidation of power and his allowing the Panama Defense Force (PDF) to act with impunity, including the killing of an unarmed U.S. service member by forces under Noriega's command. Events like these provided the justification first for an increased U.S. military presence, and then for U.S. military action to take Noriega into custody and to put in power the elected but never seated government of President Guillermo Endara.

The United States had the following objectives for OJC:

- Protect American lives (nearly 30,000 U.S. citizens resided in Panama at the time)
- Bring Noriega to justice
- Neutralize the PDF
- Ensure implementation of Panama Canal Treaties
- Protect the 142 U.S. defense sites in Panama
- Restore Panamanian democracy.[2]

On December 20, 1989, operating under the authority of the Commander of the U.S. Southern Command (SOUTHCOM), Joint Task Force-South (JTF-SOUTH) managed and led the operation with a combined force of 22,000 Soldiers, 3,400 Airmen, 900 Marines, and 700 Sailors.[3]

Shortly after the successful launch of OJC, which lasted under a month, the United States launched the planned follow-on stabilization initiative, Operation PROMOTE LIBERTY (OPL) to secure Panama in the wake of chaos and looting in some cities and support efforts to restore services and reconstitute the PDF in a new, democratically controlled security sector. Despite OPL being a military creation, its planners made every effort to make it an IA effort once the operation got underway. While this was more than partly due to a realization of deficiencies in planning, the military was able to adapt quickly. The SOUTHCOM Joint Plans Officer (J-5) was named commander of the new Civil Military Operations Task Force (CMOTF), which was placed under the operational control of the U.S. Chargé d'Affaires in Panama.[4] The CMOTF began work under OPL on December 22, 1989. OPL ran parallel with OJC for a short period and continued its work after OJC concluded on January 11, 1990. OPL (and CMOTF by extension) was expected to support the requirements identified by the Embassy team and the new government of Panama. The intent for some level of civil-military coordination, which was not apparent during the planning stage of OPL, can be seen by CMOTF being brought under operational control of the U.S. Chargé d'Affaires. Although CMOTF was nominally under the U.S. Chargé d'Affaires and a new Panamanian government had been established, neither the understaffed Embassy nor the new Panamanian government had the required capacity or plans for managing a complex stabilization operation.

Initially, CMOTF personnel were combined with active duty soldiers and reservists.[5] Shortly thereafter, MP companies joined four Brigade Task Forces from the 82nd Airborne Division and 193rd Infantry Brigade to reinforce OPL. The U.S. military brought in MP and infantry units to help calm the cities under OPL and left residual forces behind after the conclusion of OJC to enable the transition back to Panamanian civilian control.

U.S. efforts in Panama had an important law enforcement component from the beginning. A key part of the mission in OJC was the apprehension of a fugitive: Manuel Noriega. The core of the stabilization mission in OPL was restoring law and order and building new civilian law enforcement capabilities. Over the course of the initial operations and their aftermath, the USG deployed at least five departments and agencies to achieve these missions. Key among these were the U.S. Department of Defense (DoD), the Department of State (DoS), and agencies of the DoJ including the Drug Enforcement Administration (DEA), the U.S. Marshals Service (USMS), and the ICITAP.

LINES OF OPERATION

The wide range of USG entities involved in Panama brought diverse authorities, resources, expertise, and cultures to a complex mission. For purposes of drawing a distinction between military and LE tasks, it is useful to consider USG involvement in terms of a number of distinct, but interrelated lines of operation (LOOs).[6]

The first LOO covers OJC, which had narrow LE lines of operation and during which larger LE needs became apparent to many involved with the mission. The second LE LOO looks at the transitional phase where there was increased need to conduct and build LE capabilities among the host nation (HN) personnel. LOO 3 reflects the transition into long-term capacity building measures. See Table 2-1.

LOO 1 **LE-Related LOOs for Operation JUST CAUSE**	1a. Noriega Extradition 1b. Detainee Warrants 1c. Passenger Screening and Airport Security
LOO 2 **Operation PROMOTE LIBERTY and Transition Phase**	2a. Maintain Law and Order 2b. Reestablish HN LE Capacity
LOO 3 **Civilian-led Reconstruction and Stabilization**	3. Building HN civilian LE capabilities

Table 2-1. Summary of Lines of Operation (LOO) for Panama.

LOO 1—LAW ENFORCEMENT-RELATED LINES OF OPERATION FOR OPERATION JUST CAUSE

Noriega Extradition.

Taking custody of Noriega and extraditing him on a federal narcotics warrant was a key objective of OJC. In the immediate pre-invasion planning, it became apparent to military planners that, although Noriega could be captured and detained by U.S. military forces, the formal arrest was an LE mission; this was eventually delegated to the USMS. A team of personnel from the USMS Special Operations Group (SOG) responded to the request for assistance from the U.S. military and deployed within a couple of days of the start of OJC.

In theory, the SOG can conduct self-sufficient operations, but in practice for this extradition mission in an overseas combat zone, they were heavily reliant on the U.S. military. The military provided the Marshals with air transport to Panama and additional logistics and related support once they arrived in country. The USMS team worked closely with the military to conduct Noriega's extradition successfully. After Noriega surrendered to U.S. Army Soldiers, he was then handed to the USMS SOG Team, which formally arrested him. USMS SOG personnel accompanied Noriega on a U.S. Air Force (USAF) C-130 flight to the United States. One of the DEA agents onboard the flight read Noriega his rights. A few weeks after Noriega was extradited to the United States, the rest of the USMS team also returned home (by the end of January 1990).

Detainee Warrants.

In addition to Noriega, there were numerous other outstanding U.S. Federal warrants for persons believed to be residing in Panama. Given the availability of sufficient SOG personnel beyond the immediate requirement for extraditing Noriega, the USMS team saw the opportunity to clear some of these warrants.[7] Clearing warrants became an important aspect of the OJC mission that, while not planned for in advance, was readily performed by deployed U.S. personnel.

Organization and accomplishment of this line of operation required close USMS and military collaboration. The USMS team worked with MPs to check the identities of prisoners of war against the warrants. Some SOG deputies accompanied the military to prisons and detention centers to seek out and arrest those with outstanding warrants issued against them.

As the detention mission was larger than expected, it became a challenge for the USMS team. The task grew to include processing several thousand detainees. Normally, U.S. personnel supporting host-nation officials would accomplish this, but the collapse of the Panamanian government left this entirely to a small group of U.S. officials.

Logistics also proved to be a challenge for an expanded USMS mission. The lack of satellite phones and vital technology such as surveillance equipment posed significant problems in conducting the tasks taken on by the USMS.

Passenger Screening and Airport Security.

Once the military secured the Torrijos-Tocumen International Airport in Panama City, it became quickly apparent that there was a need to extend screening for wanted persons to passengers traveling in and out of the airport. This task fell primarily to USMS personnel who were already screening detainees for outstanding warrants. The USMS team began to screen passengers traveling through the airport to ensure that they were not among those on USG wanted lists and to prevent the smuggling of contraband. MP canine units supported the search for contraband. The USMS team also maintained coordination and communication with the DEA and Federal Bureau of Investigation (FBI).

One of the challenges to conducting passenger screenings resulted from the technology that was used to convey the wanted lists. The warrants were sent to the USMS team in the form of computer printouts, and the team looked through reams of printouts during the identification process at the airport. The Emergency Operations Center (EOC) at USMS Headquarters in Washington, DC, helped the team run names of detainees through databases so that the team on the ground could either clear or formally arrest those being detained on suspicion. The procedure involved long periods of processing time since the USMS had to conduct most of the checks manually. The team members sent details and fingerprint cards to Miami for analysis and database checks.

Only after the U.S. Embassy was back up and running could the USMS team use computers to access the National Crime Information Center (NCIC) database and other resources, which helped the team accomplish its tasks more efficiently.

The military provided airport security (U.S. Army Rangers provided perimeter security) while agents from the USMS, DEA, and FBI operated inside. Some MPs and regular army personnel conducted static post and roving patrols inside the airport premises (including MP dog handlers). MPs also manned checkpoints at the airport's perimeter. Basic airport security by the military was well within standard doctrine and the MPs and other units were well equipped for this line of operation.

LOO 2—OPERATION PROMOTE LIBERTY AND THE TRANSITION PHASE

Though highly successful militarily, OJC sparked several days of looting and relative anarchy in Panama for which the United States and the newly empowered democratic Panamanian leadership was unprepared. The original plan for stabilization in Panama called Operation BLIND LOGIC (and renamed OPL) was developed by the military as a civil affairs operation in support of the U.S. Embassy and Panamanian government. The plan assumed an Embassy team and new Panamanian government would have the capacity to work together with the military to accomplish OPL. Although they would ultimately have operational control over the mission, the State Department and Country Team had no role in the planning of OPL. Within the military uneven integration was also a problem: OPL was begun shortly after OJC was launched and ran parallel with OJC for a short while. However, these two operations were not planned to easily integrate with each other.[8] This revealed a significant gap in U.S. planning, which had not adequately taken the challenges of post-combat efforts into account. But as the circumstances on the ground demanded it, SOUTHCOM initiated the J-5 led Civil Military Operations Task Force (CMOTF) under OPL and used improvised measures to address challenges related to the lack of HN civilian capacities. The CMOTF, which was not staffed to address law and order issues,[9] focused on coordinating the restoration of basic services, organization of government departments and standing up ministries.

However, with law and order remaining in a precarious situation the U.S. military also took measures to deal with this challenge. The military established the U.S. Forces Liaison Group (USFLG) and Judicial Liaison Group (JLG) to take on the tasks of training and setting up a new police force to address the issues in maintaining law and order[10] and standing up the court systems. By early January 1990, with a host of ad hoc bodies functioning in Panama, the Commander, U.S. Special Operations Command, proposed the establishment of a Military Support Group (MSG) to bring the CMOTF and all SOUTHCOM and JTF-SOUTH organizations involved with the civil-military operations under a single command. The MSG was stood up under SOUTHCOM on January 17, 1990, with support from Psychological Operations (PSYOPS), Civil

Affairs (CA), the Police Force Liaison Division (PFLD, the former USFLG), the Joint Special Operations Task Force (JSOTF), and Military Police Brigades.[11]

Under at least formal U.S. Embassy control, which was part of the effort to create some level of civil-military coordination, the CMOTF, USFLG, and eventually the MSG assumed the entire range of government functions, acting on behalf of the government where no local capability existed and transitioning long-term capacity building to U.S. civilian organizations and the Panamanian government. In the LE arena, two supporting lines of operation led or supported by U.S. military and civilian organizations can be discerned (Maintain Law and Order, and Reestablish Host Nation LE Capability). The analysis below looks at how U.S. entities were prepared to conduct these two supporting LE lines of operation and what types of coordination occurred.

Maintain Law and Order.

In the immediate aftermath of the launching of OJC, it became apparent that the HN lacked both law and order and civilian capacities. Since the CMOTF did not have the capability to conduct this larger mission on its own, the U.S. military, as the only entity in the country with the capacity to provide the level of stability required, had to deal with the lack of a viable and functioning HN security and LE apparatus. While some of the military personnel through the CMOTF concentrated on reviving civilian capacities, the military set up the USFLG to deal with law and order issues. Absent a clear and defined mission set with relevant authorities and solid planning and doctrine, the military pieced together available authorities in a combat situation to stand up interim structures to plug critical gaps.

From January through June 1990, approximately 200 U.S. army personnel patrolled the streets of Panama City and the outlying provinces to maintain order. The new Panamanian government with U.S. assistance screened former PDF personnel and after weeding out those who were known to have been corrupt or violated human rights, incorporated the screened personnel into the new forces.[12] When these new Panama National Police (PNP) personnel became available, the U.S. military began to conduct joint patrols with them.[13] At first the U.S. Army personnel were mostly general-purpose forces (GPF), and included a minority of MPs and reservists/National Guard who were police in civilian life. The GPF were untrained for the tasks of either providing law and order or partnering with local forces. The MPs had LE training, but were not trained in community and related policing skills.[14] The MPs, using available resources and personnel, filled-in gaps relating to law and order until the ICITAP program started to graduate recruits of the new PNP academy able to take over some of these duties by themselves. MPs provided installation law enforcement, quick reaction forces, protective services, and inner-city courtesy patrols.[15] By mid 1990, the training program was being conducted by the ICITAP, while the military continued joint patrols with HN police.

(Re)-Establish Host Nation Law Enforcement Capacity.

An urgent task for the United States and the newly-installed Panamanian government was to set up a new police force consisting of vetted former PDF personnel in the wake of the PDF's collapse. At the outset, U.S. forces were effectively an occupying force. To get beyond this dynamic, the military had to ensure the mobilization of a Panamanian government-supported police and a functioning judicial and penal system. The challenges as with the other LOOs began with the planning phase. OPL was designed to run for only 30 days—in this case until late January 1990. By then, U.S. forces had begun to address the breakdown in law and order by securing the country. Despite this achievement, there were inadequate numbers of local Panamanian forces out on the streets providing security, so the U.S. military had to address this issue.

The USFLG assisted the Panamanian government in setting up the Panamanian *Fuerza Publica* (Public Force) and oversaw its division into the PNP, air service and maritime service, investigative arm, immigration service, port police, presidential guard, and prison guards. The USFLG ensured that the Public Force began to deploy vetted forces by the end of January 1990.[16] The USFLG also coordinated equipping and setting up the prison system and set up the JLG under a U.S. Army South (USARSO) civilian international lawyer tasked with getting the court system functioning again.[17] Under its immediate task of setting up a new police force to address law and order issues, the USFLG began to work on getting HN personnel to assume this task. As such, one of the USFLG's first activities under its key task of addressing enforcement and maintenance of law and order was to develop a basic 20-hour curriculum for a transition training course for the HN forces, which it later transferred to the MSG (the USFLG became the Public Force Liaison Division under the MSG when the latter body was set up in January 1990).[18] The development of the course by the

USFLG was not ideal, but the staff found reservists who were police officers in their civilian lives to help shape it.

Once established, the MSG took over the multiple efforts of entities like the CMOTF and USFLG and became the body that formulated a strategy for restoring basic government functions, reconstituting security services, and bringing order to the many ad hoc efforts underway. By the end of January 1990, civil-military efforts had succeeded in providing security to the point that U.S. infantry forces could redeploy to the United States.[19] But even this was probably premature. Though the MSG was stood up with a view to a 1-year mission, it depended heavily on CA reservists. Because the reserves had not been called up, the CA reservists' tours continued to be 30-day tours, causing chronic staffing problems.[20]

As a means of reconstituting the PNP, the MSG used MPs to administer the 20-hour basic police training course to PNP personnel.[21] In February 1990, Congress invoked the Section 660 of the Foreign Assistance Act (FAA) of 1961 which limits U.S. assistance for the training of foreign police, causing the military to curtail the training of the PNP. The U.S. military continued to mentor the PNP under an FAA Section 660 provision that permitted the use of residual security assistance funds to equip a police force. The MSG was left in a difficult situation—with no civilians to transition the mission to and restricted authority for providing direct support to police efforts in Panama, the urgency to find a civilian answer increased. The DoS approached the ICITAP to advise and support the transition of the former PDF into the new PNP. Before this, the ICITAP had not been involved in a capacity and skills building program on this scale. This led to several changes within the ICITAP and its training doctrine.[22] With the Panama mission, the ICITAP's role was broadened through a special congressional authorization in February 1990, allowing the agency to implement a comprehensive reconstitution and training program for the PNP.

Once again, the organizational work was under civilian control (in this case, placing the Deputy Chief of Mission [DCM] in charge of the CMOTF). The ICITAP would run the programs and be in charge of training, and the MSG would conduct operations, including joint patrols with the Panamanian Forces. The MSG continued to provide mentors and to monitor the PNP and other forces through joint patrols, and officially ended its involvement with the PNP in June 1991.[23]

The military proved able to adapt to overcome organizational chaos and several gaps in doctrine, training and shortfalls in personnel, particularly the failure to mobilize reserve civil affairs units early on. But all of these areas could have been addressed with consultations and preparations with civilian counterparts in the preoperational planning stages before OPL got under way.

LOO 3—CIVILIAN-LED RECONSTRUCTION AND STABILIZATION

Prior to 1989, the ICITAP's standard operating procedures were mostly limited to delivering training in criminal investigations, forensics, and administrative and management capabilities in relation to career advancement for federal law enforcement bodies. It could not provide lethal equipment or deliver training or assistance in relation to arrests, use of force, and related police techniques. After Congress changed the

ICITAP's mandate, the task of training and setting up the PNP was handed over to the ICITAP, which gradually began to take over from the MSG and the MP-led efforts to reconstitute and train the PNP.

Building Host Nation Civilian Law Enforcement Capabilities.

In January 1990, the ICITAP was tasked to develop a 2 1/2-year project plan to assist in the restoration of LE in Panama through the development of the PNP and Judicial Technical Police (PTJ). The ICITAP was granted $13.2 million through several congressional authorizations, including the Urgent Assistance for Democracy in Panama Act and supplemental funds.[24] Prior to Panama, the ICITAP had never deployed personnel permanently in support of its training operations. The ICITAP manager hired U.S. contractors[25] to conduct initial training and field evaluations.

The 20-hour MSG-run basic police course continued for a short while, as the ICITAP prepared for the handover. The MSG worked towards building a basic national police and managed through the creative use of certain legal provisions to give the new police uniforms and other basic equipment. The collapse of the PDF had allowed vehicles and equipment to be misappropriated or destroyed, so the U.S. military had to provide everything for new recruits, including transportation.

Apart from logistical and administrative support and some planning in early stages after it took over the training of the PNP, the ICITAP did not coordinate or work with any military. The MSG continued to conduct joint patrols, but as Panamanian forces grew, MSG involvement shrank.

Other agencies, including the DEA, played a role in providing substantial assistance to counternarcotics units and operations of the Panamanian police. The Legal Attaché Office at the Embassy, which also represents the FBI, worked with the PNP on cases that were of interest to the United States (but did not provide the police with assistance).[26]

Between 1990 and 1999, the United States provided more than $43 million to help enhance the capabilities of Panamanian judges, prosecutors, investigators, and public defenders and their organizations. The U.S. Agency for International Development (USAID) provided about $9.6 million in rule of law assistance to help improve judicial institutions, while the ICITAP provided about $33.7 million to support the establishment and strengthening of a national police force.[27]

OBSERVATIONS AND RECOMMENDATIONS

The observations from the research were grouped into seven main thematic areas. In this section, a series of recommendations follows each observation statement.

1. Coordination / Planning.

There was a lack of interagency planning to coordinate the full force of the U.S. Government capabilities, expertise, responsibilities and authority to respond to complex operational needs.

At the strategic level, coordination and planning in relation to the Panama mission revealed some unevenness in thinking about overall objectives and consideration of second- and third-order effects of operations. There were gaps in the allocation of roles for tasks that required interagency involvement. Despite the fact that Noriega's arrest was a primary mission objective, military planners did not build a relevant LE response element into the original plan.

Shortly after the launch of OJC, the DoD requested the USMS to conduct Noriega's arrest and extradition and additional LE requirements that occurred after the initial combat phase of the mission. After just a few days, the PDF was successfully dismantled, and the U.S. military wrested all control of the country from Noriega supporters, enabling the new government to assume power. However, the USG planners had not taken the potential for civil chaos into account. Planning had focused primarily on the military-led combat operations. The dismantling of the PDF left a security vacuum in the domestic security apparatus, and there was a planning deficit in relation to dealing with the possible effects of this security vacuum. The military was ordered to destroy all PDF-related infrastructure during military operations and to dismantle the remaining PDF after the cessation of combat operations.

After combat operations ended, the military had to rebuild infrastructure and provide equipment for the new PNP. The cascade effect of this gap in planning led to MPs having to move quickly to provide infrastructure and support to the PNP in the short-term until civilian LE agencies were capable of taking over the task of reorganizing and training the police.

There is a direct correlation between strategic planning gaps and the pointed lack of IA planning prior to the Panama mission. Most of the planning was conducted by the military. The inadequate IA planning and coordination also meant that there was no entity allocated to deal with civilian LE and RoL needs such as revitalizing the police, justice and corrections systems. The military stepped in and formed ad hoc bodies like the Justice Liaison Group, consisting of USARSO lawyers, to support the Panamanian courts, and the Civil Military Operations Task Force and U.S. Force Liaison Group to manage the transition. The U.S. civilian and LE agencies that arrived in the country after the end of combat operations spent a considerable amount of effort to work with these entities and transition to a civilian-led recovery and stability operation.

Recommendations:

1.1. Institute a comprehensive, flexible, coordinated IA strategic planning framework with clear role allocation, valid contextual assumptions, and related IA responsibilities and capabilities.

1.2. Create a common LE entity and LE planning framework to respond to the range of LE requirements.

1.3. Account for funding availability and restrictions during the planning stage.

1.4. Create capacity in civilian organizations for "overhead teams" with the ability to conduct assessments and provide oversight and relevant operational expertise before and during operations.

1.5. Consider whether the DoS Office of the Coordinator for Reconstruction and Stabilization (S/CRS) Civilian Response Corps could resolve some of these issues.

2. Organizational Capability.

No one organization had the authority/capability to rehabilitate or create host nation law enforcement entities.

With the Panama mission, the ICITAP's role was broadened through a special congressional authorization in February 1990, allowing the organization to implement a comprehensive reconstitution and training program for the PNP. The new and broadened mandate forced a change in the ICITAP's core doctrine, and it was compelled to undergo rapid reorientation in terms of its mission and operational tasks.

The military assumed LE tasks and capacity building in the interim as ICITAP personnel began arriving in the country and setting up operations. The initial MP-led training focused mainly on providing the new PNP with basic skills relating to law enforcement. The training focused on civil order, patrolling, searches, and detention. The MPs did not have the doctrine and requisite capacity to provide additional training like community policing.

The lack of a selected USG LE agency to plan and implement training and capacity building also resulted in systemic gaps such as the lack of a standard process to vet the new PNP personnel. The ICITAP, which took over the task from the MPs, found that it had to re-vet some of the personnel as the procedure had been conducted in ad hoc fashion by the MPs, who mainly used existing police rosters that were located in some of the police stations to assist in the vetting process. Unlike during the Panama operation, there are now several agencies that conduct LE-related tasks, both at the operational and capacity building levels. While no one agency conducts a full suite of LE training and capacity building, the USMS, the ICITAP, the Department of State's Narcotics Affairs Section (NAS), and a range of other agencies and departments conduct capacity building and training in investigations, forensics, witness and judicial security, eradication, and interdiction-related operational tasks.

The responsibility for different elements of LE lies with several departments including the DoJ, the DoS, and the USAID. Oversight and control of these various agencies is fragmented. While there have been many improvements in IA cooperation in international operations, some of the fundamental problems that arose during the Panama effort continue.

Recommendation:

2.1. Create an official lead agency or entity with designated authority and capacity to conduct LE-related tasks with the coordination and support of other Departments and Agencies as relevant.

3. Command and Control.

Different approaches to command and control (C2) exhibited by military and law enforcement.

The flexibility permitted in the internal authorities of LE agencies allowed for these agencies to widen or narrow the scope of their operation with minimal internal debate or need to review authorities. The USMS, for example, was able to take on additional tasks (within its accepted scope of work), at short notice with minimum formal procedure. The statutory authority given to LE agencies gave the USMS team leader the ability to interpret the specific circumstances and respond. The military, in turn, despite more formal authorities, was able to set up structures with mandated leadership and hierarchies like the CMOTF and USFLG to react to the requisite needs.

However, all these adaptations were ad hoc and based on the extent of flexibility available to the entities in question. This raises several issues in relation to having the military assume civilian tasks, or even of having multiple civilian agencies with overlapping roles and responsibilities. Faced with unforeseen requirements, the various U.S. agencies adjusted their procedures and organization; but not in close coordination with one another. Although the DCM was notionally in charge of the effort, the bodies like the USFLG and JLG set up by the military had more control over specific actions and plans. With the creation of a JLG, for example, the provision of advice to the justice-sector was largely in the hands of an expert hired by the military without consultation with civilian agencies. The command and control relations were left vague, and informal coordination worked relatively well in Panama, but the process was less than optimal.

Recommendations:

3.1. Define C2 in advance and clearly articulate and convey it to personnel who need to execute the operation.

3.2. Structure training, education, and increased interagency exchanges to promote understanding about available capabilities, responsibilities, roles, and limitations in relation to C2 and Rules of Engagement (ROEs).

3.3. Develop a system of command relationships and trigger points for when military and LE occupy and alternate between supporting/supported roles.

3.4. Conduct clear assessments of host nation C2 capability to ensure that military and civilian agencies have the necessary information to make relevant operational decisions.

4. Operational Sustainability.

Most civilian agencies lacked organic logistics and were dependent on the military for key logistic and communications support.

USG civilian agencies lacked organic logistics for this operation, and there were no existing arrangements for support from the military (which did end up providing all critical support). Agencies, such as the USMS in Panama, did not have logistics outside of their team equipment and capabilities. The gaps meant that the operators had to spend a considerable amount of time and effort organizing these aspects once in theater. The military was able to provide much of the needed support and assistance, but on an ad hoc and often personality-dependent basis.

Many agencies depended on the military to provide airlift, ground transport, accommodation, and other necessary support. Nonmilitary organizations also depended on the military for secure communication. LE agencies like the USMS mostly used secure military communications platforms to contact and communicate with USMS headquarters. Once the U.S. embassy reopened, the USMS team was able to use the communications through the embassy as well. In both cases, the need for civilian secure communications was not planned for in advance and depended on available military capabilities.

Recommendations:

4.1. Pre-arranged agreements for military support to civilian organizations for contingencies should include pre-established points of contact (POCs) to deal with logistics and lines of communication prior to deploying. Also ensure the POCs are made aware of future plans and are able to work together prior to a crisis deployment.

4.2. Set up an IA system of early identification of elements (capabilities, logistics, and support) in theater.

4.3. Educate the military on capabilities available outside the military and what is required to support the organizations providing those capabilities.

4.4. Require interoperability across IA operating systems, communications platforms, etc., to enable coordination of efforts (and staff and technical placements).

5. Operational Planning.

Gaps in the planning process were responsible for an inability to harness expertise across the IA to establish a comprehensive operational plan.

At the time of OJC, there were few formal mechanisms established to manage and conduct IA communication and planning (such as National Security Policy Directive [NSPD] 44, DoD Instruction 3000.05). The consequences of a lack of an IA planning process became obvious early in the operation—a gap in LE-related planning, in particular, proved to be the most difficult to overcome. Planning for Panama was mostly conducted by the military, which focused on the combat operation. Despite the lack of a plan for the follow up operation, the military was able to maintain order in response to the domestic security vacuum created by the dismantling of the PDF. The MPs who had the closest and most compatible skills with civilian agencies assumed the burden of training in the short term until they were able to hand off to the ICITAP.

The lack of access to useful intelligence/general information about the environment, organizations, and individuals led to incorrect assumptions prior to the Panama operation. The lack of civilian planning meant that information and intelligence generated mostly pertained to the PDF and locations and support for U.S. military bases to the exclusion of key law enforcement or other civilian-related indicators. This was a failure that affected all the agencies working in the country. The planning gap that left out IA expertise meant that skills and capabilities needed for reconstruction and stabilization efforts were introduced on an ad hoc basis.

Recommendations:

5.1. Ensure that agencies communicate and coordinate to enable clarity of purpose and establish mission objectives and are able to create the necessary "buy-in" across the IA.

5.2. Ensure flexible funding to allow agencies to undertake collateral duties in addition to planned mission tasks.

5.3. The country plan should address RoL objectives and milestones in coordinating an integrated approach—not just "laundry lists."

5.4. Consider a "Federal Coordinating Officer"[28] model to include liaison ability across the IA.

6. Operational Coordination.

Few pre-existing and organized mechanisms exist for integrating operations by different agencies.

The lack of standard integration mechanisms was apparent from the start of the Panama operation. Those efforts that worked in theater were mostly ad hoc. Again, the initial lack of combined planning set the stage. When the embassy was reopened and the country team began establishing its presence, there was inadequate communication and coordination with the military and the country team, which was expected to take over civilian tasks.

Recommendations:

6.1. Clearly articulate roles/objectives in general and standardize them for specific operations. Consider leveraging people who have worked together in missions and on deployments.

6.2. Have an agreed, binding system for dispute resolution and a dedicated person to manage authority (e.g., POC with authority).

7. Capacity Building.

There was a varied range of authorities, expertise, entities, and capabilities for rebuilding host nation law enforcement.

Due to the absence of any other entity capable of reconstituting the HN police at the end of combat operations, the military assumed the task. Some civilian LE agencies like the FBI, provided limited assistance in screening former PDF personnel. However, the military did not have formal background in or preparation for such large-scale capacity building outside of Special Operations Forces. Using available authorities, including temporary authorities, the military set up ad-hoc entities like the USFLG and the JLG. Again, this was not an area in which the military had doctrine, training, or other preparation.

The military was also the only entity available to provide support and assistance to HN law enforcement entities. MPs provided training that was based on their capabilities and doctrine, and military advisors tried to work with civilian ministry officials. While the training led by the MPs was a suitable interim response, there remained a need for a civilian agency with the relevant capabilities to accept the task. In the absence of such an agency, one had to be allocated and created. The ICITAP was brought into the operation and provided with a congressionally-approved mandate change to reconstitute the HN police. But even this did not provide a well-prepared response since the mission was new to the ICITAP.

Without organizations with the right authorities and resources, the lack of preparation led to waste of both resources and labor. The military had to provide assistance and support and also delay the redeployment of many of its personnel because the needs on the ground could not be met without U.S. military support.

Recommendations:

7.1. Include capacity building as a primary component in military and civilian plans.

7.2. Include assessment of the HN criminal justice environment in pre-operation planning to enable understanding of problem space and response design.

7.3. Benchmarks from the USG to inform military actions should include criteria for an exit plan. There must be IA agreement on benchmarks, which should be regularly reassessed/revised as relevant.

7.4. Determine supported-supporting relationships between USG agencies in relation to working with HN agencies.

7.5. Ensure prior assessment of the impact of disbanding/neutralizing HN LE and HN extant capability.

CONCLUSION

The Panama operation revealed some significant challenges that USG agencies continue to grapple with at varying levels across different operations. The challenges inherent in **IA planning and C2** within and between agencies underlie many of these issues. The lack of combined, clear and responsive planning between civilian and military agencies revealed some crucial gaps, which are not limited to the Panama operation. While subsequent efforts through presidential mandates and agency-level efforts like the creation of S/CRS have succeeded in improving the IA planning process, gaps remain and often become critical in post-conflict settings.

At the operational level, the organizational, structural, and tasking differences between LE and military agencies suggest ways that coordination could support the larger mission effectively. The different ROEs and C2 between military and LE highlight the different ways the two types of entities react to emerging challenges in theater. Reasonably flexible authorities provide LE entities, like the USMS, the ability to react to situations with minimal senior leadership guidance, while the military response is accompanied by semi-formal or formal structures that are hierarchical, strictly guided and mandated by leadership. This does not stop the military from adapting, but it means the most durable military adaptation is structural and is institutionalized from the top down, often involving the creation of new organizations rather than just changes in behavior or tasks. Bottom up adaptation in the military from tactical innovation and informal decisions made by individual commanders and soldiers is often effective, but generally ad hoc and not immediately incorporated into practice. The inherent adaptability of both LE and the military, as illustrated through the case of Panama, revealed the ability of such entities to work together in dynamic environments. Without clear operational tasking, however, redundancies, overlap and even conflict are more likely. While the

Panama operation does not provide the optimal example for military-LE coordination, it reveals some significant possibilities for collaboration on LE-type tasks. The civilian LE agencies and the military collaborated to secure the airport and screen passengers. Detainee processing by all accounts worked well as LE agencies and the military through ad hoc measures worked out their roles in relation to this task.

The other crucial area is **defining and allocating LE roles** prior to an operation. While the military can and has stepped into many contexts to conduct LE-related tasks in the absence of any alternatives, the clear pre-allocation of LE roles and capabilities in a new mission would help operational preparation and bring the appropriate capabilities into theater more efficiently. Most stabilization-type operations now demand a strong LE component since a wide array of countries that require such interventions have inadequate or poor LE capabilities that cannot easily be used to support a mission, even when the overall objective is supporting and building up the host nation's LE system. The LE component requires a wide range of tools to conduct short and long-term capacity building for a HN.

Prior allocation of **operational requirements** through POCs is also crucial to any operation and the Panama operation revealed some crucial gaps in this area that needed to be addressed. Improved and consistent measures to maintain communications, logistical coordination, support and interoperability should be prioritized among the agencies. Pre-planned agreements on communication platforms, logistics and agency-wide integration at the operational level have the potential to help overcome systemic problems that often undermine responses to complex operations.

The Panama example provides a clear illustration of the capabilities that were required.

A **transition plan** that takes into account the changing roles and responsibilities and a strong grasp of contextual needs and capacities should be institutionalized as part of the IA process. This should include discussion of capabilities that need to be introduced to maintain sustainability of an operation if the environment demands it. Consideration of formalizing overhead/advance teams is another recommendation that could prove key to complex operations and enable closer military and civilian LE cooperation. A designated agency or group of agencies, which are mandated and structured to provide LE advice, assistance, and long-term capacity building, is increasingly relevant.

See Table 2-2 for summary of Panama observations and recommendations.

	OBSERVATIONS	RECOMMENDATIONS
1) Coordination and Planning	There was a lack of interagency planning to coordinate the full force of the U.S. Government capabilities, expertise, responsibilities and authorities to respond to complex operational needs.	1.1 Institute comprehensive, flexible, coordinated IA strategic planning framework with clear role allocation, valid contextual assumptions, and related IA responsibilities and capabilities. 1.2 Create common LE entity and LE planning framework to respond to the range of LE requirements. 1.3 Account for funding availability and restrictions during the planning stage. 1.4 Create capacity in civilian organizations for "overhead teams" with ability to conduct assessments, and provide oversight and relevant operational expertise before and during operations. 1.5 Consider whether the S/CRS Civilian Response Corps could resolve some of these issues.
2) Organizational Capability	No one organization had the authority/capability to rehabilitate or create host nation law enforcement entities.	2.1 Create an official lead agency or entity with designated authority and capacity to conduct LE-related tasks with the coordination and support of other Departments and Agencies as relevant.

Table 2-2. Summary of Observations and Recommendations from Panama.

3) Command and Control	Different approaches to command and control (C2) exhibited by military and law enforcement.	3.1 Define C2 in advance and clearly articulate and convey it to personnel who need to execute the operation. 3.2 Structure training, education and increased interagency exchanges to promote understanding about available capabilities, responsibilities, roles and limitations in relation to C2 and ROE. 3.3 Develop a system of command relationships and trigger points for when the military and LE occupy and alternate between supporting / supported roles. 3.4 Conduct clear assessments of host nation C2 capability to ensure that military and civilian agencies have the necessary information to make relevant operational decisions.
4) Operational Sustainability	Most civilian agencies lacked organic logistics and were dependent on the military for key logistic and communications support.	4.1 Pre-arranged agreements for military support to civilian organizations for contingencies should include pre-established POCs to deal with logistics and lines of communication prior to deploying. 4.1 (a) Also ensure the POCs are made aware of future plans and are able to work together prior to a crisis deployment. 4.2 Set up an IA system of early identification of elements (capabilities, logistics, and support) in theater. 4.3 Educate the military on capabilities available outside the military and what is required to support the organizations providing those capabilities. 4.4 Require interoperability across IA operating systems, communications platforms, etc. to enable coordination efforts [and staff and technical placements].
5) Operational Planning	Gaps in the planning process were responsible for an inability to harness expertise across the interagency to establish a comprehensive operational plan.	5.1 Ensure that agencies communicate and coordinate to enable clarity of purpose and establish mission objectives and are able to create the necessary "buy-in" across the IA. 5.2 Ensure flexible funding to allow agencies to undertake collateral duties in addition to planned mission tasks. 5.3 The Country plan should address RoL objectives and milestones in coordinating an integrated approach—not just "laundry lists." 5.4 Consider a "Federal Coordinating Officer" model to include liaison ability across the IA.
6) Operational Coordination	Few pre-existing and organized mechanisms exist for integrating operations by different agencies.	6.1 Clearly articulate roles/objectives in general and standardize them for specific operations. Consider leveraging people who have worked together in missions and on deployments. 6.2 Have an agreed, binding system for dispute resolution and a dedicated person to manage authority (e.g., POC with authority).
7) Capacity Building	There was a varried range of authorities, expertise, entities, and capabilities for rebuilding host nation law enforcement.	7.1 Include capacity building as a primary component in military and civilian plans. 7.2 Include assessment of the HN criminal justice environment in pre-operation planning to enable understanding of problem space and response design. 7-3. Benchmarks from the USG to inform military actions should include criteria for an exit plan. There must be IA agreement on benchmarks. which should be regularly reassessed/revised as relevant. 7-4. Determine supported-supporting relationships between USG agencies in relation to working with HN agencies. 7-5. Ensure prior assessment of the impact of disbanding/neutralizing HN LE and HN extant capability.

Table 2-2. Summary of Observations and Recommendations from Panama. (Cont.)

ENDNOTES - CHAPTER 2

1. President George H. W. Bush, Address to the Nation on Panama Invasion, *New York Times*, December 20, 1989, available from *www.nytimes.com/1989/12/21/world/fighting-panama-president-transcript-bush-s-address-decision-use-force-panama.html*.

2. John T. Fishel, *The Fog of Peace: Planning and Executing the Restoration of Panama*, 1992, p. 4, available from Defense Technical Information Center Web Site, *oai.dtic.mil/oai/oai?verb=getRecord&metadataPrefix=html&identifier=ADA251124*; Wiliamson Murray, ed., *Transformation Concepts for National Security in the 21st Century*, September 2002, p. 392, available from Strategic Studies Institute of the U.S. Army War College Web Site, *www.strategicstudiesinstitute.army.mil/pubs/display.cfm?PubID=252*; Ronald H. Cole, *Operation Just Cause: Planning and Execution of Joint Operations in Panama February 1988 – January 1990*, 1995, p. 29, available from Small Wars Journal Web Site, *smallwarsjournal.com/documents/justcause.pdf*.

3. Cole.

4. Major William J. Conley, Jr., (USMC), *Operations Just Cause and Promote Liberty: The Implications Of Military Operations Other Than War*, Thesis, 2001, p. 21, available from Small Wars Journal Web Site, *smallwarsjournal.com/documents/conley.pdf*.

5. Richard H. Shultz, *In the Aftermath of War: U.S. Support for Reconstruction and Nation Building in Panama Following Just Cause*, Maxwell Air Force Base, AL: Air University Press, 1993, p. 29, available from Air University Press Web Site, *aupress.maxwell.af.mil/books/Shultz_Aftermath/Aftermath.pdf*.

6. This is not to suggest that the USG involvement was planned in this way or even that the USG managed its involvement in Panama in terms of LOOs. Rather, the LOOs are presented here purely as a (*post facto*) means to understand the continuity and breadth of ways in which LE contributed to achievement of USG objectives in Panama. See Qualifications and Limitations section on p. 4 for the explanation on how this study formulated the Lines of Operation.

7. After arriving in Panama, the USMS team leader cleared with USMS headquarters and the DoJ the expansion of their intended role from just facilitating and conducting Noriega's extradition to include looking for fugitives.

8. Lawrence A. Yates, *The U.S. Military's Experience in Stability Operations 1789-2005*, Fort Leavenworth, KS: Combat Studies Institute Press, 2006, p. 18, available from U.S. Army Combined Arms Center Web Site, *www-cgsc.army.mil/carl/download/csipubs/yates.pdf*.

9. Shultz, p. 29.

10. *Ibid.*

11. Conley, pp. 11, 21-22.

12. ICITAP Panama Project Evaluation Report, Washington, DC: Office of Planning, Evaluation and Audits, 1992, p. 8.

13. *Ibid.*, p. 20.

14. Two augmentation companies and a platoon-size unit of National Guard soldiers supported MP commitment well into 1991. These included the 534th and 549th MP companies, which combined operations under the 92nd MP Battalion.

15. Stephen J. Green, *Augmentation Units in Panama, Military Police PB 19-93-1*, Fort Leonard Wood, MO: U.S. Army Military Police Corps, June 1, 1993, p. 11.

16. Murray, pp. 222-223.

17. John T. Fishel, *Civil Military Operations in The New World*, Westport, CT: Praeger Publishers, 1997, pp. 70-71.

18. Shultz, p. 37.

19. James H. Embrey, "OPERATION JUST CAUSE: Concepts for Shaping Future Rapid Decisive Operations," in Murray, pp. 222-223.

20. Shultz, p. 16.

21. ICITAP Panama Project Evaluation Report, p. 20.

22. Shultz, p. 48.

23. ICITAP Panama Project Evaluation Report, p. 20.

24. *Ibid.*, pp.1-2, 19.

25. These were mostly bi-lingual former FBI and LE officers.

26. National Center for State Courts, *ICITAP/Panama Police Training Project Evaluation – Final Report*, Arlington, VA: National Center for State Courts, August 23, 1994, p. 9.

27. Government Accountability Office, *Foreign Assistance: U.S. Rule of Law Assistance to Five Latin American Countries*, Washington, DC: Government Accounting Office, August 1999, p. 5, available from *www.gao.gov/archive/1999/ns99195.pdf.*

28. See 41 USC 5143, Sec 5143. A Federal Coordinating Officer is appointed by the President to coordinate federal assistance in the event of a major disaster or emergency.

CHAPTER 3

COLOMBIA

INTRODUCTION

Much of the U.S. Government (USG) interest in and response to the law enforcement (LE) situation in Colombia was driven by domestic U.S. concerns about the increasing influx of cocaine to the United States in the 1980s and concerns about imminent state failure in Colombia in the late 1990s. Initial USG assistance efforts in Colombia, which focused primarily on eradication and interdiction, evolved into comprehensive LE, Rule of Law (RoL) and economic and community development efforts as the USG and Colombian governments refined and improved their approach over time.

Colombia offers several unique lessons, especially in relation to successes and challenges in long-term LE training and capacity building efforts across the USG interagency (IA). The current efforts consist primarily of combined USG agency responses that deliver skills building, training, mentoring, and advice to a range of host nation (HN) military and LE agencies; that provide equipment and intelligence, technical and development support; and that involve USG-led, but HN executed, combined military and LE efforts.

A close study of USG involvement in Colombia reveals that a range of wide-scale and comprehensive efforts, which are the results of long years of trial and error, have been successful in developing Colombian LE capabilities and RoL systems, and improving governance. The Colombia example shows the value of a comprehensive, long-term commitment to a partner nation and highlights successes of years of involvement and increasingly well-integrated USG IA efforts. Colombia also reveals the value of a HN government taking the lead in developing its capabilities and running operations. USG efforts in Colombia depend on HN commitment to improving security and development and the political will to make necessary changes within the HN domestic system.

However, as the core narcotics problem is being addressed, other emerging challenges that demand an improved LE/RoL response are coming to the fore. Among these is the growing problem of criminal gangs (*Bandas Criminales Emergentes* [BACRIM]), consisting of former paramilitaries and other criminals. These well-armed gangs have experience and links with drug cartels and the Revolutionary Armed Forces of Colombia (FARC). This emerging threat to LE and RoL is showing similar characteristics to the development of the FARC. In the late 1980s and early 1990s, as drug cartels were attrited under consistent U.S.–backed Colombian military and LE operations, the FARC, which was then a revolutionary insurgent group, began to take over the drug trade. The Colombians, with U.S. support, then began to target the FARC. Initially, the Colombian government followed the same strategy it had used with the drug cartels: target areas controlled by the cartels, destroy their operations in that area, and move on to the next one. This strategy did not work well with the FARC. Each time the government vacated an area, the FARC would move back and punish anyone from the civilian population suspected of helping the government. This increasingly alienated the civilian population, making people reluctant to help the government undermine the FARC. Comprehensive measures that combine security and development like the Colombian Strategic Development Initiative (CSDI) are responses to the morphing nature of the FARC threat. Adapting a more sophisticated response, the Colombian government began to establish security and a permanent presence in areas wrested back from the FARC. The government then began to introduce baseline public services to these areas, many of which were located deep in rural areas with little infrastructure and access to basic services. As this strategy began to show some success, the Colombian government, with U.S. assistance, has begun to extend it across a wider geographic area.

The FARC and now BACRIM reveal the manifest challenges of insurgency, which is often followed by more traditional organized crime and related challenges. As an insurgency dies down and basic services are established, many former fighters may turn to crime, especially if economic opportunities are inadequate and LE remains weak. Where the drug cartels and the FARC were cohesive organizations, the BACRIM consists of diffuse networks with links to many criminal outfits and well-armed criminal gangs. The Colombian military, which led operations against the FARC, believes the BACRIM is an LE problem that needs to be dealt with by the Colombian National Police (CNP). The CNP, however, remains under capacity and is yet unable to successfully take on the BACRIM. This suggests the need to shift resources and attention to the police quickly as progress is made against the FARC.

While there are many qualitative successes in Colombia, fundamental challenges, such as a viable solution for the BACRIM, remain and need to be addressed in the long term, including Colombian capabilities in relation to managing their own efforts without U.S. assistance and U.S. domestic concerns about ongoing support for Colombia.

This section contains the following areas: (1) A synopsis of the Colombia operation and LE Lines of Operation; (2) Observations drawn through research and interviews; and (3) Recommendations drawn through the validation process.

SYNOPSIS (1989-PRESENT)

Plan Colombia emerged out of the Andean Counter-Drug Initiative (ACI), which was launched in 1989 to provide military, economic, and law enforcement aid to Bolivia, Peru, and Colombia. U.S. officials launched the ACI in response to the vast amount of drugs that were being smuggled into the United States from these three countries. In the late 1990s, the USG was facing realistic fears that Colombia was not only becoming the biggest coca producing country in the region, but could possibly come apart with the government under siege by drug cartels. As a result, the United States approved a focused joint effort with Bogota known as "Plan Colombia," which was a diplomatic, military, LE, and economic engagement, initially with a heavy focus on narcotics trafficking through interdiction and eradication.

Former Colombian President Andres Pastrana initially developed Plan Colombia as a 5-year (2000-05) plan, with the objectives of ending Colombia's long armed conflict, eliminating drug trafficking, and promoting peace, security, and economic and social development. However, Plan Colombia,[1] while undergoing changes over the years, continues in the present with no significant break in U.S. support. The primary U.S. objective in supporting Plan Colombia was to prevent the flow of illegal drugs into the United States. The United States also had a strong interest in helping

Colombia promote peace and economic development because that would contribute to regional security.

U.S. support for Plan Colombia began in 2000, when Congress passed legislation providing $1.3 billion for the region in interdiction and development assistance over 5 years.[2] The Colombian government drafted the initial strategic plan with support from many U.S. agencies, resulting in a process and a plan with broad U.S. commitment.

For implementation, American and Colombian officials formulated an Interagency Action Plan. The focus for the first 2 years of the Plan specifically targeted regions in the country that were considered high-threat areas. The new measures were expected to reduce coca production by 50 percent within the initial 2 years. The U.S. plan included five components of proposed assistance:

- Improving governing capacity and respect for human rights
- Expansion of counternarcotics operations in Southern Colombia
- Alternative economic development
- Increased interdiction in Colombia and the region
- Assistance for the Colombian National Police.[3]

For the U.S. side, the relevant departments and agencies followed the doctrinal directive set out in Presidential Decision Directive 73 (PDD 73), which remains classified but mandated closer IA coordination and planning.[4] The planning that resulted from PDD 73 is often cited as an example of successful IA coordination. The Executive Committee (EXCOMM) was a direct result of PDD 73. The EXCOMM, comprised of Assistant Secretary-level representatives from the

Office of National Drug Control Policy (ONDCP), the U.S. Agency for International Development (USAID), and the Departments of State (DoS), Justice (DoJ), Defense (DoD), Treasury (DoT), and Commerce (DoC), was set up to plan and discuss with the Colombian government how to best support its efforts.[5] By many accounts, the close IA coordination generated by this process led to a solid plan and integrated USG effort for assisting Colombia. The initial plan included strong stabilizing measures, followed by economic and social development. The plan set out funding and objectives of the various agencies early in the process. The largest funding components were allocated to the counternarcotics and interdiction operations.[6]

Among the agencies' concerns were LE needs, the need for a new code of justice in Colombia, ways to respond to and mitigate money laundering, and, of course, how to undermine and prevent vast drug trafficking networks. Over the years, human rights, justice, and peace have come to undergird the provision of assistance. The U.S. Congress continues to direct that U.S. agencies do not work with military/police units that are associated with human rights violations, and Congress makes funding conditional on observing human rights. At the inception of Plan Colombia, using interagency cooperation, agencies divided and took up key tasks and agreed to collaborate on others.

When work on U.S. support to Plan Colombia began, the DoS was designated the lead U.S. agency, with Western Hemisphere Affairs (WHA) and International Narcotics Affairs and Law Enforcement Affairs (INL) functioning as the key bureaus. Currently, INL continues to coordinate DoS LE assistance for Colombia, while WHA helps formulate policy and integration across the interagency. DoS continues to control funding for most of the civilian and LE-related projects, and coordinates programs with other departments and agencies including the DoD, DoJ, USAID and DoT.

From the program's inception, the DoD continues to manage large programs in the provision of U.S. support for Colombia, both for operational support and specific types of training. The DoD conducts its tasks in coordination with other agencies and though State is the lead agency, the Military Group (MilGroup) in the U.S. Embassy Bogotá manages Defense counternarcotics support.[7]

After the DoS and DoD, the agency that plays a significant role in Plan Colombia, particularly in relation to LE efforts, is the DoJ. The department is involved in training and capacity building for the entire Colombian LE and justice system. Some DoJ agencies such as the Federal Bureau of Investigation (FBI), the Drug Enforcement Administration (DEA) and the Bureau of Alcohol, Tobacco, Firearms, and Explosives (ATF), conduct their operations independently of Plan Colombia funding and within their organizational structures. Some of these same agencies also provide varied amounts of training to Colombian LE personnel. In such instances, they often collaborate with other USG agencies.

USG support to Colombia involves ongoing collaboration among several DoJ entities, including the Narcotics and Dangerous Drugs Section; the Office of International Affairs; the Asset Forfeiture and Money Laundering Section; the Computer Crimes and Intellectual Property Section; the U.S. Marshals Service (USMS); the FBI; the Office of Foreign Assets Control (OFAC); the ATF; and the DEA. The DoJ has a full-time staff based in Bogotá to oversee and manage their assistance programs. Each of the agencies has an attaché at the embassy and works within the Country Team. Currently, the Office of Overseas Prosecutorial Development Assistance and Training (OPDAT), the International Criminal Investigative Training Assistance Program (ICITAP), the USMS, INL's Narcotics Affairs Section (NAS), and the MilGroup manage the bulk of training, technical assistance and capacity building to HN LE personnel as part of Plan Colombia, through various security assistance and support tools.

The USAID works mostly on development programs and has a full-time staff based in Bogotá to oversee and manage their assistance programs, which include economic and social assistance to Internally Displaced Persons and farmers. The USAID also provides some support to RoL programs through institution and capacity building efforts.[8]

Since 2000, U.S. support to Colombia has undergone several changes. Initially, significant funding and U.S. efforts were directed towards coca eradication and interdiction of drug producers and traffickers. In the years since, the U.S. Congress adjusted the focus of these efforts in the budgets, and in 2008, Congress mandated more work on "soft side" issues like human rights and RoL. As a result, project funds for the USAID and the DoJ increased in the last year.[9]

In 2003, following the election of President Alvaro Uribe, the Colombian Government expanded its security component of Plan Colombia (PC) to include a "clear, hold and consolidate" strategy under Uribe's "Defense and Democratic Security Policy."[10] Its objective was to establish a government presence and control over the entire country, especially in areas affected by armed groups and drug traffickers. Expanded authority provided by the U.S. Congress coincided with this emphasis in Colombian Government security strategy and allowed U.S. agencies to support the clear, hold, and consolidate strategy.[11] As this strategy matured, the government of Colombia implemented additional follow-on strategies. In January 2007, it announced the "Plan Colombia Consolidation Phase (PCCP),"[12] with the goal of consolidating gains made under the Defense and Democratic Security Policy through continued military action and increased social and economic development programs. The Colombian government pledged to provide $44 billion while U.S. support involves approximately $4 billion for fiscal years 2007 through 2013. During this period, the United States intends to and has begun a slow drawdown and handing off of many of the ongoing assistance programs to Colombia.[13]

U.S. support for Colombia's current strategy, the CSDI,[14] combines a synchronized and comprehensive approach to securing areas, providing policing and public services in tandem with economic and social development projects. The CSDI relies on three main USG entities: the MilGroup, the NAS, and the USAID. Under the CSDI, these USG entities alternate with each other in leading USG support to Colombian efforts. To implement the CSDI, the country is divided into regions and, depending on the level of security needed for each region, one of these agencies takes the lead support role with Colombian counterparts and agencies. For regions that require a strong military/LE response, the MilGroup takes the lead in providing support and assistance to the Colombians. If the level of need is related towards eradication of extensive coca cultivation, then the NAS takes the lead on the U.S.-side and provides support to the Colombians with their eradication and interdiction efforts. In areas that have a stable security situation and an increased government presence in the form of police stations and small courts, the USAID takes the lead in providing necessary support to set up economic and community development projects alongside Colombian ministries and regional actors (see Figure 3-1).

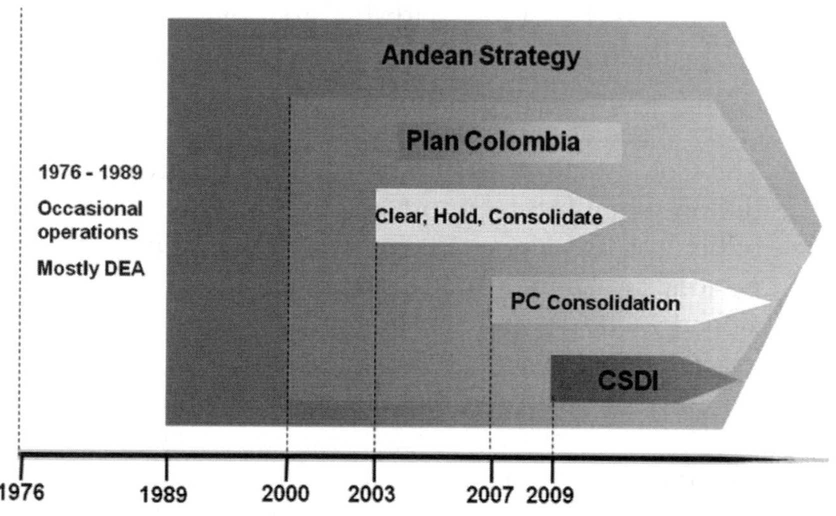

Figure 3-1. Timeline and Key USG-Colombia Strategies.[15]

Between 2000 and 2008, the U.S. Government has provided $6 billion in aid to Colombia ($4.8 billion to reduce illicit narcotics and increase security; $1 billion for Social and Economic Justice and $239 million to promote rule of law).[16]

There is a formal IA coordination mechanism in relation to Plan Colombia, with all U.S. agencies, through long practice, reporting to the chief of mission. Weekly Deputy Chief of Mission (DCM) meetings are held at the embassy to coordinate PC support and include discussion on oversight of PC funding.

DEA chairs a separate meeting, which focuses mostly on operations-related LE.

LINES OF OPERATION

Plan Colombia involves a complex program of assistance, technical support, capacity, and institution building that ranges across all local agencies and involves as many as 20 U.S. departments and agencies, some working directly through PC funding and guidance, others with their own funding lines (including DoD counternarcotics funds), but still operating within the USG goals for the country. For purposes of drawing a distinction between military and law enforcement tasks, it is useful to consider USG involvement in terms of a number of distinct, but interrelated lines of operation (LOOs).[17] This section describes the three major LOOs identified: (1) Counter narcoterrorism operations; (2) LE training; and (3) Capacity and institution building. See Table 3-1.

LOO 1 **Counter Narcoterrorism Operations**	1a. Aerial/Manual Eradication and Interdiction Operations 1b. U.S.-Led Maritime, Aerial, Riverine Interdiction and Support 1c. Border Security 1d. LE Response o Judicial Wire Intercept (Wiretap) Program o Use of Extraterritorial Laws to Prosecute Drug Crimes
LOO 2 **LE and RoL Training**	2a. ICITAP General Purpose LE Training/FBI, DEA Training 2b. USMS Witness Security and Judicial Security Training
LOO 3 **Capacity and Institution Building**	3a. Legal Reform, Mentoring and Advising

Table 3-1. Summary of Lines of Operation (LOO) for Colombia.

LOO 1 - Counter Narcoterrorism Operations.

One of the key tenets of U.S. assistance to Colombia is the provision of equipment, training, and support to the Colombian military and police to conduct combined operations to eradicate coca fields and interdict drug producers and traffickers. The level and extent of USG support and training provided to interdiction and eradication efforts in Colombia is unique to the region. While the USG provides assistance to other countries in the region, Colombia is the recipient of the majority of funds, equipment, training, support, and technical assistance. The U.S. strategy in Colombia involves providing targeted commando training, interdiction training, aerial surveillance, and technical assistance to Colombian security forces. These efforts include facilitating Colombian military and police joint eradication operations. In some instances, U.S. LE agencies collaborate with the Colombian police by providing intelligence and information in addition to technical assistance and non-lethal equipment. This many-layered eradication and interdiction strategy is supported by the involvement of several U.S. agencies, which provide support and training through combined efforts. In addition, the U.S. agencies conduct and support maritime and riverine interdiction efforts and pursue the use of robust extraterritorial laws to extradite and prosecute narcoterrorists.

Aerial/Manual Eradication and Interdiction Operations.

Aerial and manual eradication and Colombian LE and military combined interdiction operations in coca growing areas is one of the mainstays of USG IA assistance efforts in Colombia. The NAS oversees eradication support operations for the CNP and works closely with the CNP's Anti Narcotics Directorate (DIRAN) by providing equipment (i.e., helicopters and fixed-wing aircraft), related logistics, and training to conduct these operations. The DEA, MilGroup, and NAS coordinate and support Colombian-led eradication and interdiction missions. The DEA and the MilGroup provide intelligence and the NAS helps coordinate operations with the Colombian Army's Counter Drug (CD) Brigade and the CNP's commando unit, known as *Junglas*. The Colombians lead the eradication missions while U.S. agencies (DEA, MilGroup) develop target packets, which they provide to the *Junglas*. The *Junglas* conduct their own planning and command and control (C2) for the mission. The CD Brigade provides ground cover for aerial eradication missions. In addition to operational support and coordinate eradication efforts, the NAS provides support (e.g., flight-related support and funding), while the CNP provides security for manual eradication. The U.S. Army 7th Special Forces (SF) Group delivers training to *Junglas* to conduct these complex operations. The DoS Office of Aviation supports the NAS to provide U.S. assistance to the CNP's Air Service (ARAVI). ARAVI provides air mobility support for a range of CNP functions including aerial and manual eradication efforts, airlift for the *Junglas,* and the provision of rotary-wing aircraft.[18]

To ensure long-term police presence in areas that have been cleared of FARC presence, the NAS and 7th SF Group train mobile squadrons of rural (*Carabineros*) police. These *Carabineros* units have established a police presence in all 1,098 municipalities in the country, the vast majority of which did not have a police presence in the past. The *Carabineros* units patrol the countryside regularly and provide a visible police presence and by extension a government presence in rural areas.

To support the police presence, the USAID and OPDAT have begun supporting the setting up of "*Casas Justicia*" (small units to deal with basic justice-related issues such as divorce, land-titling, etc.) in cleared areas. These combined U.S. supported efforts have improved security in conflict areas and also provide vital information and support to Colombian efforts at extending government presence to rural areas.

U.S.-Led Maritime, Aerial, Riverine Interdiction, and Support.

In addition to combined IA efforts to assist HN agencies, the U.S. military and LE agencies conduct maritime and aerial interdiction operations, engage in related intelligence-gathering efforts, and provide support and training to riverine interdiction efforts. SOUTHCOM and the Joint Inter-Agency Task Force-South (JIATF-S) support a range of maritime and aerial LE interdiction operations by providing coordination, logistics (aerial warning and control system [AWACS], aircraft, frigates, personnel, assistance with training, and liaison with military from other countries), C2, communications, and intelligence through operations centers to U.S. and Colombian LE/military agencies. The JIATF-S integrates its efforts with foreign LE agencies in other countries in the region to enable it to identify, monitor, track, and hand over targets to LE agencies in these countries, depending on the location of the arrest. Most often U.S. Coast Guard (USCG) law enforcement detachments[19] are embedded with U.S. Navy frigates to ensure that the boarding team includes an LE team rather than only military personnel. The JIATF-S also coordinates and pools resources with other nations (including co-locating personnel from other nations within the JIATF-S) and with USG agencies like Customs and Border Protection (CBP). The JIATF-S also uses military platforms to convey information to multiple countries in real time and coordinate responses to ensure successful interdiction. The USCG attaché in Bogota and the JIATF-S, work together closely to provide information and liaison assistance to USCG teams, especially in relation to high seas intercepts. The JIATF-S collaborates with the DEA and the USCG to interdict smugglers using submersible craft while the DEA and the MilGroup collaborate on Tactical Analysis Teams (TATs) (all source intelligence fusion teams) to pursue drug traffickers. The military provides logistics and intelligence support while the DEA brings its authorities/intelligence efforts to assist the military in these operations. Agencies such as the DEA maintain synergies with the MilGroup and FBI, and communicate regularly with the U.S. embassy's defense attaché and judicial attaché and collaborate on extraditions, serving arrest warrants, and related legal advice. Through these multi-layered efforts, the USG has been able to regularly detain, arrest, and prevent large numbers of cocaine shipments in transit zones from reaching the United States.

In addition to these efforts, the NAS supports the Colombian Air Force with its Air Bridge Denial Program, which works on intercepting small aircraft used by drug smugglers. The NAS provides training in maintenance, logistics systems and equipment. Due to the Air Bridge Denial Program's high level of success, it has been extended to provide maritime surveillance.[20] The Colombian navy gets assistance from the MilGroup and the CBP through training and support to improve its ability to patrol the vast networks of rivers in the country and conduct riverine interdiction operations.

Border Security.

Providing border security assistance and support is another area where U.S. Agencies are increasingly collaborating and orienting their efforts. Colombia shares 6000 kilometers of land borders with five countries and seaboards overlooking the Caribbean Sea and Pacific Ocean. In addition, the country has a vast network of rivers that are increasingly being used by traffickers to smuggle drugs out of the country. Securing Colombia and preventing drug trafficking is a massive challenge. Various USG agencies work with DIRAN, Airport Police, and private seaport operators to prevent narcotics trafficking and the smuggling of contraband items, explosives and counterfeit currency through Colombia's seaports and airports. Immigration and Customs Enforcement (ICE) and the CBP work, with the NAS to deliver training and technical assistance to improve the ability of Colombian border control agencies to combat drug trafficking, money laundering, contraband smuggling, and commercial fraud. Through these programs, U.S. agencies deliver training in counternarcotics capabilities, passenger processing, rail interdiction, and container security measures.[21]

In addition, the NAS provides funds for a port security initiative, which is a combined effort between the Colombian government, the CNP and private industry. Through this initiative, port employees receive training, support and logistical assistance including offices and equipment to conduct port security.

Law Enforcement Response.

A strong USG-backed combined LE and military strategy has supported Colombia to move its Counternarcotic/Counter Drug campaign from a purely national security/military focused effort, to focus on using more LE measures against criminals and narcoterrorists. This change of strategy has provided Colombia with enhanced abilities and access to diverse means to prosecute drug cartels, rising numbers of criminal gangs, organized crime, and the FARC. However, USG agencies and the military are concerned over the rising levels of organized crime and the demands on the HN police to respond to the new types of criminal outfits (e.g., BACRIM). The CNP remains under capacity to deal with organized crime, and the Colombian military is reluctant to engage these groups as they consider the BACRIM and other criminals an LE issue. USG personnel working with the CNP have indicated that the CNP needs to build up its operational/tactical capabilities further (intelligence, weapons, airpower, manpower, and other resources) if it is to take on these groups and provide an LE response to the challenge.

Judicial Wire Intercept Program. The DEA-led Judicial Wire Intercept Program is a U.S.-Colombian combined LE effort against drug cartels and criminals. Through this program, the DEA trains and mentors Colombian LE personnel to conduct wiretapping and related investigations. The DEA's International Drug Flow Attack Strategy (IDFAS), which was implemented to actively disrupt drug flows to upend the drug market, is a key component of the U.S. LE agencies' counternarcotics strategy. The DEA, operating under 21 USC 959/960 and Act 960 A of the Patriot Act, uses the Judicial Wire Intercept Program as one of its primary operational tools in implementing the IDFAS. Neither of these Acts requires the crime committed to necessarily have a nexus in the United States, which gives the DEA wide latitude to accomplish the IDFAS strategy. The DEA works with DIRAN's Heroin Task Force on bilateral heroin investigations and has incorporated Sensitive Investigations Units (SIUs) (which include vetted national police personnel) and works to dismantle criminal organizations by gathering and using evidence that can be upheld in U.S. and Colombian courts. Through these and related efforts, the DEA and Colombian authorities have succeed in gathering vital information to arrest, extradite and convict drug traffickers.

Use of extraterritorial laws to prosecute drug crimes. The USG utilizes a range of extraterritorial laws to prosecute drug-related crimes committed outside the United States. This has provided an effective LE tool for U.S. federal agencies to take action (offensive judicial action rather than defensive) against the FARC and related criminals and narcoterrorists. USG agencies work closely with Colombian agencies to prosecute transnational criminals, narcoterrorists, and drug cartels.

In particular, 21 USC 959/960 and Act 960A of the Patriot Act are useful in these efforts since these laws do not require commission of defined acts to have a nexus with the United States. These have facilitated extraditions of wanted persons; the use of the Judicial Wire Intercept Program; and have provided the ability to use evidence gained through wiretaps in U.S. courts. The ability to share some of the relevant technology with vetted/trusted Colombian police has led to successful operations.[22] The vetted units and the LE measures that are currently being used and expanded have provided the Colombians with a vastly expanded set of tools to target the FARC and other criminals. USMS efforts to extradite wanted criminals to the United States have provided vital leverage for Colombian and U.S. LE, and has created a deterrent effect among Colombian narcoterrorists. In addition, the Office of Foreign Assets Control (OFAC) conducts civil investigations to target drug traffickers and their businesses, and uses the "Clinton List"[23] to develop sanctions against Colombian criminal entities. The OFAC collaborates with the DEA and ICE to identify targets. Colombian banks and LE take action based on these sanctions to pursue drug traffickers' extended support networks. OFAC synchronizes its activities with the CNP, vetted units of the Directorate of Judicial Police and Investigations (PIJIN), and the *Fiscalia General de la Nacion* (National Prosecutor's Office) to leverage all their capabilities against the drug traffickers. The OFAC has sanctioned the FARC as a narcotrafficking organization using the "Kingpin Act"[24] rather than using Global War on Terror legislation. The Kingpin Act has provided the OFAC with an expanded ability and an effective means to target the FARC, its supporters, and enablers. The OFAC also works closely with Colombian asset forfeiture organizations to support and assist them in asset forfeiture efforts targeting drug traffickers and their associates.

LOO 2—LAW ENFORCEMENT AND RULE OF LAW TRAINING

When Plan Colombia was launched, Colombian police and courts were prone to high levels of corruption and ineffectiveness that resulted in impunity for drug traffickers. Addressing these systemic problems in the Colombian RoL system while building basic LE/RoL capabilities is a key focus of U.S. assistance. Since 1999, the USG has trained more than 70,000 police and military personnel.[25] The restructuring of the judicial system is closely related to efforts aimed at improving LE. Several of the U.S. agencies involved in these efforts collaborate and work closely to ensure the work complements their efforts.

Through the provision of general purpose and specialized training, the ICITAP and USMS continue to provide the bulk of LE-related training for Colombian LE agencies. A range of USG agencies provide varied levels of training to HN LE agencies through joint and specialized training as relevant. The OPDAT provides oversight and policy and budgetary direction to both ICITAP and USMS programs.

While U.S. agencies deliver a range of training and capacity building measures, overall training program priorities are set or changed based on joint review and decisions of the U.S. and Colombian governments.

ICITAP General Purpose Law Enforcement Training / FBI, DEA Training.

The provision of general and specialized LE training for Colombian police is a cornerstone of USG efforts to support and reinforce local LE and improve HN police capabilities to conduct effective LE. The USG agencies involved in these efforts also deliver training on how to work with the RoL system.

The ICITAP delivers training to CNP investigators (patrolmen and crime scene investigators) on basic skills such as gathering evidence and providing testimony; this training directly addresses a fundamental gap in local police capabilities. The ICITAP collaborates with other agencies such as the DEA to conduct Undercover Operations Training Courses for trusted units of CNP personnel. The ICITAP also provides training for several other agencies including, the National Prosecutor's Office and the Administrative Department of Security (DAS, the Colombian Security Service). In addition to training and technical assistance to the Colombian police and other LE entities, the ICITAP provides equipment that can be used in investigations, communications gear and a limited number of vehicles to some of the Colombian agencies. Other USG Agencies including the USMS, ATF, and ICE collaborate with the ICITAP to deliver training as relevant to HN LE agencies.

USMS Witness Security Training and Judicial Security Training.

In the past, witnesses and the Colombian judiciary have been heavily targeted for violence and killings by drug cartels and the FARC. The USMS delivers training through the Judicial Security (JudSec) and the Witness Security (WitSec) Training Programs to close off some of the big gaps in relation to HN LE capabilities to address these challenges. The USMS trains CNP, the National Prosecutor's Office, DAS, and CTI (Investigations Unit of the National Prosecutor's Office) personnel in the provision of protection for, and facilitating relocation of judiciary personnel and witnesses. In addition to protection measures, the USMS also trains Colombian personnel in threat assessment and management and other logistical considerations that are involved in ensuring closure of cases. The USMS also provides vehicles, bulletproof vests, and other nonlethal equipment to the trainees.

LOO 3—CAPACITY AND INSTITUTION BUILDING

From the inception of Plan Colombia, the DoJ has advocated building a strong justice system to stabilize and develop RoL in Colombia. There is continuous dialogue between the DoJ and the U.S. Congress to renew funding, and the changed funding measures over the years have reflected the growing recognition of the need to develop a comprehensive Colombian RoL and justice system. At the start of Plan Colombia, funding for justice sector reform was in the range of $ 6-7 million; currently this has been increased and is now between $25-30 million.

Legal Reform, Mentoring, Advising.

Assistance and support on legal reforms and justice sector development is another important aspect of U.S. efforts in Colombia. This assistance is primarily provided by the OPDAT (the primary DoJ agency with doctrine and capability to conduct justice sector institution building, technical assistance and training for foreign countries). OPDAT support is primarily delivered through technical assistance, institution and capacity building for the Justice Sector Reform Program (JSRP). The OPDAT manages and coordinates the subordinate Technical Assistance Program (TAP) for the JSRP as well. This support and assistance extends to training, mentoring, and advice. The OPDAT works closely with other U.S. LE agencies and HN counterparts, especially the National Prosecutor's Office and the CTI, and maintains a close relationship with the Colombian Ministry of Justice to identify trainees.

One of the singular achievements of this comprehensive legal reform assistance effort is Colombia's transition to a new Criminal Procedure Code (which changed the existing inquisitorial system into an accusatory system of justice).[26] The transition was completed in January 2008. There is a direct correlation between the new system and the increase in public satisfaction in the judiciary due to open trials and new transparency in the system. Part of the OPDAT's implementing capabilities consists of the provision of technical advice by Resident Legal Advisors (RLAs) to their Colombian counterparts to implement this new Code of Justice, to strengthen the Colombian judiciary, and to enhance the courts' working relationships with other criminal justice sector institutions. In addition, the OPDAT collaborates with agencies such as the Internal Revenue Service (IRS) and the ICE to conduct joint training on anti-money laundering measures and also collaborates with the USAID to support victim assistance efforts as part of implementation of the new code of justice. The DEA has supported changes to the law that allow more robust use of HN undercover agents, and the FBI's Criminal Investigations Division supports the DAS through capacity building and mentoring for vetted units.

OBSERVATIONS AND RECOMMENDATIONS

The observations from this research have been grouped into six main areas. In this section, a series of recommendations follows each observation.

1. Planning and Formal Mechanisms
2. Capacity Building: Institutional Reform and Advising
3. Relationship Between Crime, Terrorism, and Drug Trade
4. Commitment to Partnership
5. Collaboration, Informal Execution
6. Relative Advantage of Running a Supporting Mission.

1. Planning and Formal Mechanisms.

Comprehensive IA planning conducted with HN and focused on HN objectives at strategic and operational levels. Plans are developed, assessed, reviewed and amended through a pre-agreed system.

USG IA planning continues to be fine-tuned with strong Colombian involvement. This has worked in current and previous capacity building efforts and continues to work in relation to new strategies like the CSDI. USG agencies ensure that the Colombians are in the lead. By all indications, the successful joint planning and program execution is a sign that the delegation of the decisionmaking process to the field staff and away from the headquarters in Washington has been effective. This is also an indication that the experience and capacity that has been built up over the years has been effective in enabling USG agencies' field staff to make the relevant decisions. This cooperation has improved at the USG IA level with increasingly close cooperation between LE and the intelligence and military communities.

The Colombian example also reveals the importance to the mission of having strong and effective personalities (both HN and USG) involved. The interactive and close cooperation between serious and honest military and LE leaders and USG agencies has succeeded in integrating planning processes and leveraging capabilities to ensure successful military and LE efforts against the drug cartels and the FARC. This joint and collaborative process has also succeeded in building HN capacities to better plan and execute a wide range of operations.

Despite these successes, there are some gaps in the long-term process such as the need to define, identify, and plan for military to LE transition and counterinsurgency (COIN) operations and to clearly identify and build the capacity of the Colombian entities that will be responsible for these activities. Currently, there are serious concerns about the rise of criminal gangs and cartels that are replacing the FARC. The BACRIM presents a new kind of challenge for LE. These groups have more firepower than regular criminal gangs and also have more experienced fighters, who have faced the Colombian military in previous encounters. However, the Colombian military, which has been the lead element in the fight against the FARC and succeeded in hastening its attrition, views the BACRIM as an LE problem. Colombian LE remains under capacity, both numerically and in relation to training and equipment, making it difficult for the police to take on the BACRIM on its own without more capacity building assistance. Questions remain about how to increase LE capacities and the role of the Colombian military in taking on this emerging challenge.

As the USG begins drawing down its assistance to Colombia, one of the frequent questions revolves around metrics. The original metrics included a 50 percent reduction in coca cultivation, which has not been accomplished. In fact, metrics based on the number of hectares eradicated have proven to be of little value. However, qualitatively, more parts of the country are secure, have a government presence through police and public services, and the FARC's ability to retake control of these areas has been reduced dramatically.

The need for realistic metrics that can be revisited and modified as appropriate over time will be important to the long-term success of the USG mission. Authorities and funding are eventually connected to such metrics and inadequate attention will lead to poor resource decisions.

Recommendations:

1.1. Establish granular, meaningful metrics early in the mission that can be shared with other similar operations (such as Plan Merida, which is U.S. support for Mexico's battle against violent drug trafficking).

1.2. Establish metrics that can gauge whether the HN Government has adequately established effective governance (including diminishing corruption) over the country.

1.3. Provide regular feedback to appropriators to ensure earmarks enhance (and do not unduly constrain) programs.

1.4. Develop more effective mechanisms to share program successes among the U.S. IA.

1.5. Plan beyond (U.S. and HN) political cycles (that can drive short-term goals) in order to prevent backsliding, and develop funding mechanisms to facilitate long-term plans.

1.6. Plan for sustainment on the ground if USG commitment is reduced and ensure that HN agencies are able to operate with limited external support.

1.7. Consider increased specialization (purpose-built units) among HN LE.

2. Capacity Building: Institutional Reform and Advising.

There are multiple elements to the capacity-building approach to include training and equiping, mentoring, institutional reform, and enabling HN capabilities. These mutually-reinforcing elements have significantly increased HN capacity, but Colombia is not yet self-sufficient.

The duration of USG active involvement in Colombia is still under consideration. The Plan Colombia Consolidation Phase involves a 6-year period during which the USG agencies plan to hand over programs to Colombian counterparts and agencies. However, there are concerns that domestic U.S. considerations may hasten the handover of some programs, which the Colombians may not be willing or able to sustain on their own. It is likely that USG agencies like the DEA, which conducts an increasingly successful Judicial Wire Tap program jointly with the Colombians, will remain engaged with HN agencies in the long-term, especially since the program's success also affects the shipment of drugs to the United States. However, other agencies involved in providing capacity and support to Colombian LE as part of Plan Colombia may have to scale back or draw down their programs in the next few years. Creating adequate capacity among the Colombians to transition programs to their control is a primary requirement, and building Colombian capabilities as needed remains a challenge.

The question of transition to the HN also brings up debate about extraditions. Many narcoterrorists and drug dealers end up in U.S. jails rather than in Colombian ones. While this has had some deterrent effects, the status quo has not resulted in an adequate build up of Colombian prisons to fully take over from the United States. Colombian prisons remain under capacity and are yet unable to take over the task of imprisoning and holding narcoterrorists, many of whom have been able to continue to operate their networks even while in prison due to Colombian prison officials' corruption and inefficiency. In addition, an option of transitioning to Colombian-led programs also brings up concerns about U.S. domestic policy regarding drugs and how it needs to be more effective to curtail demand in the United States.

In addition, USG agencies' ability to use expanded authorities to engage in counterinsurgency training and support has improved Colombians' ability to take on the narcoterrorists and other criminal elements. However, the need to renew these authorities each year is not a smooth process and sometimes results in USG agencies having to suspend their work until the authority is renewed in Congress. This is another aspect of the USG-Colombian cooperation process that needs to be reviewed to accommodate transition to the Colombians.

Recommendations:

2.1. Conduct holistic security sector assessment to be able to better identify and articulate the needs around transitioning programs to the HN through a strong build-up of HN capabilities.

2.1.(a). Ensure that all concerned parties understand the *cost-benefit analysis* and required length of efforts.

2.2. Analyze legitimate concerns and defend against false or inflated accusations of human rights violations, which are sometimes used by political opponents (and even illegitimate entities like narcoterrorist and insurgent groups) to undermine HN LE and military personnel and could potentially influence how the USG will set conditions for a transition.

2.3. Build and improve HN institutions' abilities to avoid and prevent human rights violations. U.S. agencies need to ensure relevant training is provided for HN police in these areas.

2.4. Make clear to U.S. policymakers the secondary and tertiary benefits of staying engaged in long-term USG LE efforts in countries that directly affect drug trafficking and related issues.

2.5. Develop capacities evenly across the spectrum of HN justice systems.

3. Relationship Between Crime, Terrorism, and Drug Trade.

Comprehensive approaches to address the nexus between narcoterrorism, the broader drug trade, and general lawlessness have proven more successful than initiatives to deal with any of these three elements in isolation.

Limiting ungoverned spaces is crucial to the policy surrounding a comprehensive approach. Isolated communities continue to be fertile areas for coca cultivation and FARC control. Increased Colombian military and LE coordination in operations has helped provide the requisite security in many remote areas of the country to enable introduction of a permanent government presence in the form of police and public services. However, there still remain areas that require security and government presence. One of the more successful initiatives in relation to setting up a permanent government presence in areas liberated from the FARC is the Center for Coordinated and Integrated Action. This unit is part of the Colombian President's office and works on coordinating and setting up government services and offices in secured areas. The comprehensive approach also involves predicting and preparing for the next iteration of the enemy. The gap in predictive analysis prevented to some extent the anticipation of smaller cartels that replaced the larger ones of the 1980s and 1990s and thereby prevented a more comprehensive response to the morphing threat. In addition to predictive shortfalls, limitations on legal authorities such as short-term expanded authorities and the inability to easily redirect funds away from tasks of original intent also make it challenging to use a flexible approach to what is a complex set of problems.

Recommendations.

3.1. From a tactical perspective, counterdrug efforts are similar to counterinsurgency efforts. Adapt these measures and training to the context.

3.1. (a) Understand and ensure that drug cartels and related problems warrant the use of LE rather than specialized tactics.

3.2. Enable skill sets that are widely applicable and adaptable, especially among HN LE, to ensure an effective comprehensive approach to narcoterrorism and general lawlessness.

3.3. Communicate more effectively to the U.S. Congress and the HN population that many of the crimes committed by various actors are connected to the narcoterrorists and their cartels and networks.

3.4. Draw more assistance from other nations that share the drug problem and related effects of diffuse cartels and criminals.

3.5. Improve understanding in relation to the demand side of the drug trade and develop domestic U.S. policy to combat the drug problem in the United States.

4. Commitment To Partnership.

A historical relationship between U.S. and Colombian agencies combined with a long-term resourced plan, reinforced by HN commitment, has resulted in significant successes.

USG efforts in Colombia are unique in comparison to many other contexts. Several USG agencies have been involved in the country for more than 2 decades, and this has built up trust and improved the ability to share information, especially in relation to LE efforts. This is especially relevant at the higher levels of the HN agencies' leadership. The DEA works with vetted units on its Judicial Wiretap Program; this was not easily achievable in the past given the large amount of HN individuals who were compromised by their involvement with the drug cartels. Many of the most successful working relationships between the USG and Colombian agencies are based on personal relationships and trust. These successes have been enhanced by strong Colombian commitment to establishing long-term relationships. However, more needs to be done especially by the Colombians to deal with corruption, which continues to have the potential to undermine these combined efforts. In addition, it is important to ensure that capable staff and the right persons are placed in jobs on the U.S.-side of the effort as well. This includes personnel with the relevant experience and ability to work across cultural barriers.

All these efforts are also closely linked to funding and political changes within Colombia. A change in the Colombian government may result in different priorities from the current one. Furthermore, inadequate funding commitments, especially from the Colombians, have adverse impacts on the long-term partnership since the USG often has to provide the bulk and mainstay of many programs.

Recommendations.

4.1. Adjust approaches based on circumstances (i.e., what level of vetting you undertake and how you work with HN units of varying levels of trust) and determine the limits to U.S. involvement with partners who may not adhere to U.S. professional ethics and standards.

4.2. Manage and include HN personnel outside of vetted units to increase capabilities of the broader government and prevent backsliding of unit cohesiveness and cooperation.

4.3. Adjust relationships to accommodate evolving U.S. financial restrictions and maintain a dialogue with the HN to establish priorities so that the HN can utilize focused support for important initiatives and make arrangements to gradually take over and manage programs on its own.

4.4. Set up additional sustainable measures to ensure competent people remain in their positions within HN agencies. Some examples of such measures include setting up a Judge Advocate General (JAG) school for HN lawyers and other measures such as ensuring that U.S.-trained HN personnel do not rotate out of their positions to prior Military Occupational Specialties (MOS) without being given the option to specialize in their position and remain at their posts, thereby preventing attrition of trained HN personnel.

4.5. Understand and accommodate the reality that U.S. doctrine and approaches do not necessarily replicate themselves exactly in foreign contexts.

4.6. Prioritize building and maintaining relationships and mentoring personnel over providing resources.

5. Collaboration, Informal Execution.

There is a high degree of collaboration within the U.S. country team and with the HN, which allows for optimized use of capabilities and resources.

The high degree of collaboration and level of personal relationships between Colombians and U.S. staff have endured despite political changes, changing governments and staff turnover. However, in some cases these arrangements remain fragile since external events, actions, and adverse statements could affect or undermine collaboration between the Colombians and the U.S. IA staff. There remains a need for even more collaboration within the U.S. Country Team in order to maximize the impact of IA support for Colombia.

One of the key areas where there needs to be more collaboration and communication between the relevant U.S. agencies is in funding. For example, many DoJ agencies, which have created direct operational benefits through foreign assistance, have to rely on other USG agencies for their funding since they do not have direct access to the foreign assistance budget. Foreign assistance authorities are limited because of the complexity of coordinating actions across the existing authorities. Having fewer entities, such as the DoS in this case, to channel requisite funds reduces the complexity involved in potentially coordinating funding and resources through several agencies. This, however, also places the DoS in the position of having to ensure that it is sensitive to other agencies' needs in foreign LE assistance to be able to adequately react to those needs.

Recommendations:

5.1. Institutionalize successful IA and HN relationships and responsibilities.

5.1.(a) Actively support specific HN individuals, mentor them, build the relationships and where possible help HN personnel succeed and rise in seniority.

5.1.(b) Ensure that there are USG officials who are capable of nurturing long-term relationships by placing them in key positions.

5.2. Ensure programming consistency and provide a sense of certainty and continuity that will enable the HN to capitalize on opportunities and active cooperation. This includes providing incentives both at institutional and personal levels.

5.3. The USG LE community needs to improve and cultivate personnel within their own agencies so that they develop strong and successful career paths that can include foreign postings, to enable successful outcomes for the USG.

6. Relative Advantage of Running a Supporting Mission.

The USG is purely an enabler in Colombia. Colombian leaders determine policy objectives and Colombian entities lead operations. This has forced the growth of Colombian capacity and assured HN ownership while allowing a relatively small USG footprint.

The USG role as an enabler has come about more by default than through a focused plan. Legislative restrictions on the USG Agencies' role in Colombia have provided the platform for them to mentor and grow relevant capabilities among the HN agencies. The small (relative to deployments of military forces) USG footprint is also the result of reluctance on the part of the USG to get inextricably involved in Colombian internal dynamics and to minimize the number of possible U.S. targets for violence. While not necessarily planned, these actions have resulted in enabling improved capacities and abilities between Colombian LE and its military, which have learned to take the lead in all operations with U.S. support. This is especially relevant in COIN operations, where it is more beneficial for the HN to be able to operate and manage the mission and tasks. The wide-scale involvement and lead taken by Colombian personnel has increased the HN agencies' legitimacy. From the perspective of the USG agencies, the legal restrictions have forced these agencies to prioritize their focus and responses. These, in turn, have ensured that the U.S. IA has focused on promoting sustainable measures such as using the training-of-trainers' method to deliver instruction enabling the Colombians to take on a wide array of tasks. This has also ensured that the USG agencies consider problems in linear fashion since an open-ended USG involvement is not necessarily guaranteed.

Recommendations:

6.1. Regularly assess HN capacity and leadership and incorporate findings into U.S. strategic planning.

6.2. Assess the expected impact of USG capacity building and reform on HN power structures and assess the threat-level and challenges inherent in retaining a small group of USG entities to provide these capabilities.

6.3. Ensure there is balance in maintaining a small footprint with support and ability to respond to threats or crises such as widespread violence.

6.4. Coordinate niche capabilities, especially among HN LE personnel, to maintain or control a situation until better-equipped or specialized forces arrive.

CONCLUSION

USG involvement in building Colombian LE capabilities involves a complex mix of IA strategies and tasks, which has resulted in relatively successful outcomes over an extended period of time. The **long-**

term involvement in that country has given the USG an opportunity to revise and fine-tune its efforts over the years. The USG's sustained efforts have created significant capacity, especially in building up skills of Colombian military and LE personnel.

The strong collaboration between USG agencies in providing combined support to HN LE and military is a key pillar of the overall effectiveness of the USG efforts. NAS and MilGroup training and equipment support and DEA/MilGroup intelligence support has been invaluable for Colombian LE and military in their eradication and interdiction efforts. The fact that USG entities **coordinate their efforts** closely in support of a common plan is a key factor in their largely successful efforts. The Colombian government's strong commitment to the partnership is another pillar in improving overall governance and security. The USG strategy of maintaining a **limited presence** in Colombia has resulted in a small and sustainable USG footprint and ensured that USG agencies' efforts focus on building up Colombian capacities through training and mentoring rather than the direct conduct of operations.

Colombia is unique among contexts where the USG is involved in several other ways, especially in relation to structural aspects. Central among these is the structure of Colombia's national police, which is under a single command structure and has authority across the country (from border to border). This has made it easier for U.S. agencies to work with the police through a comprehensive and coordinated set of training and skills building measures. In addition, police personnel are regularly moved from one area to another making it harder for the FARC and other drug cartels to co-opt or coerce individual police personnel. This has provided many opportunities to develop the police and reduce corruption (though it remains a significant problem). In addition to the operational strategy, the U.S. policy and related approach to Colombia has been strong in its consistency of commitment despite the long duration, successive changes in U.S. administrations, and evolving domestic considerations. None of these have seriously affected or undermined U.S. commitment to Colombia.

However, without a longer term view, especially in relation to the Colombian police who face the full force of the BACRIM, the United States could see years of progress start to slip. USG programs continue to deliver training and assistance to the Colombian police, but they should likely be expanded as military support is reduced. More police and additional training for Colombians will be needed for them to reach a point of self-sustainability with the police able to deal with the BACRIM and other threats.

In addition, Colombia continues to need support to build niche capabilities and investigative capabilities to maintain or control crises until better-equipped or specialized forces can be positioned, and to be able to drive prosecutions effectively. Police intelligence capabilities are also important for sustainable progress. Most USG agencies have taken a long-term view, with the idea of maintaining their relationships in Colombia over decades. Programs like the DEA's Judicial Wiretap Program and the OPDAT-supported overhaul of the Colombian justice system will give Colombia resilient and effective institutions over time. In fact, Colombians are already being called on to advise other developing nations in LE and counter narcotics given their recent success.

There also needs to be more focus both at the strategic and operational level on support to the Colombian Navy, which, while having a large jurisdiction (all national waterways come under its purview), remains (like the police) under capacity. As drug smugglers increasingly look to alternative routes to airborne smuggling, the internal river network is fast emerging as the next geographical front in interdiction efforts and the Colombian Navy is in the frontline of these efforts.

Furthermore, the United States should continue to support Colombia in prioritized areas to secure the gains made against the FARC and narcotraffickers. Ongoing assessments should look at the security sector as a whole and define needs according to local contexts.

At the IA level, it is useful to analyze and further scope out the benefits of maintaining a small footprint and presence, while providing assistance and enabling HN capabilities. The successful collaboration between the DEA, the MilGroup, and the NAS in providing targeted intelligence, assistance, advice, and equipment to the HN police and military are among successful U.S. efforts that merit further analysis and possible replication and institutionalization for USG LE assistance.

See Table 3-2 for a summary of Colombia observations and recommendations.

	Observations	Recommendations
1) Planning and Formal Mechanisms	Comprehensive IA planning conducted with the HN and focused on HN objectives at strategic and operational levels. Plans are developed, assessed, reviewed and amended through a pre-agreed system.	1.1. Establish granular, meaningful metrics early in the mission that can be shared with other similar operations (such as Plan Merida). 1.1 (a) Establish metrics that can gauge whether the HN Government has established adequately effective governance (including diminishing corruption) over the country. 1.2 Provide regular feedback to appropriators to ensure earmarks enhance (and do not unduly constrain) programs. 1.2 (a) Develop more effective mechanisms to share program successes among the U.S. interagency. 1.3 Plan beyond (U.S. and HN) political cycles (that can drive short-term goals) in order to prevent backsliding, and develop funding mechanisms to facilitate long-term plans. 1.4 Plan for sustainment on the ground if USG commitment is reduced and ensure that HN agencies are able to operate with limited external support. 1.5 Consider increased specialization (purpose-built units) among HN LE.
2) Capacity Building: Institutional Reform and Advising	There are multiple elements to the capacity-building approach to include training and equiping, mentoring, institutional reform, and enabling HN capabilities. These mutually-reinforcing elements have significantly increased HN capacity, but Colombia is not yet self-sufficient.	2.1 Conduct holistic security sector assessment to be able to better identify and articulate the needs around transitioning programs to HN through a strong build-up of HN capabilities. 2.1 (a) Ensure that all concerned parties understand the cost-benefit analysis and required length of efforts. 2.2 Analyze legitimate concerns and defend against false or inflated accusations of human rights violations, which are sometimes used by political opponents (like narcoterrorist and insurgent groups) to undermine HN LE and military personnel and could potentially influence how the USG will set conditions for a transition. 2.3 Build and improve HN institutions' abilities to avoid and prevent human rights violations. U.S. agencies need to ensure relevant training is provided for HN police in these areas. 2.4 Make clear to U.S. policy makers the secondary and tertiary benefits of staying engaged in long-term USG LE efforts in countries that directly affect drug trafficking and related issues 2.5 Develop capacities evenly across the spectrum of HN justice systems.
3) Relationship Between Crime, Terrorism, Drug Trade	Comprehensive approaches to address the nexus between narcoterrorism, the broader drug trade, and general lawlessness have proven more successful than initiatives to deal with any of these three elements in isolation.	3.1 From a tactical perspective, Counter Drug efforts are similar to Counter Insurgency efforts. Adapt these measures and training to the context. 3.1 (a) Understand and ensure that drug cartels and related problems warrant the use of LE rather than specialized tactics. 3.2 Enable skill sets that are widely applicable and adaptable, especially among HN LE, to ensure an effective comprehensive approach to narcoterrorism and general lawlessness. 3.3 Communicate more effectively to the U.S. Congress and the HN population that many of the crimes committed by various actors are connected to the narcoterrorists and their cartels and networks. 3.4 Draw more assistance from other nations that share the drug problem and related effects of diffuse cartels and criminals. 3.5 Improve understanding in relation to the demand side of the drug trade and develop domestic U.S. policy to combat the drug problem in the U.S.

Table 3-2. Summary of Colombia Observations and Recommendations.

4) Commitment to Partnership	A historical relationship between U.S. and Colombian agencies combined with a long-term resourced plan, reinforced by HN commitment has resulted in significant successes.	4.1 Adjust approaches based on circumstances (i.e. what level of vetting you undertake and how you work with HN units of varying levels of trust) and determine the limits to U.S. involvement with partners who may not adhere to U.S. professional ethics and standards. 4.2 Manage and include HN personnel outside of vetted units to increase capabilities of the broader government and prevent backsliding of unit cohesiveness and cooperation. 4.3 Adjust relationships to accommodate evolving U.S. financial restrictions and maintain a dialogue with the HN to establish priorities so that the HN can utilize focused support for important initiatives and make arrangements to gradually take over and manage programs on its own. 4.4 Set up additional sustainable measures to ensure competent people remain in their positions within HN agencies. Some examples of such measures include setting up a JAG school for HN lawyers and other measures such as ensuring that U.S.-trained HN personnel do not rotate out of their positions to prior Military Occupational Specialties (MOS) without being given the option to specialize in their position and remain at their posts, thereby preventing attrition of trained HN personnel. 4.5 Understand and accommodate for the reality that U.S. doctrine and approaches do not necessarily replicate themselves exactly in foreign contexts. 4.6 Prioritize building and maintaining relationships and mentoring personnel over providing resources.
5) Collaboration, informal execution	There is a high degree of collaboration within the U.S. country team and with the HN, which allows for optimized use of capabilities and resources.	5.1 Institutionalize successful IA and HN relationships and responsibilities. 5.1 (a) Actively support specific HN individuals, mentor them, build the relationships and where possible help HN personnel succeed and rise in seniority. 5.1 (b) Ensure that there are USG officials who are capable of nurturing long-term relationships by placing them in key positions. 5.2 Ensure programming consistency and provide a sense of certainty and continuity that will enable the HN to capitalize on opportunities and active cooperation. This includes providing incentives both at institutional and personal levels. 5.3 The USG LE community needs to improve and cultivate personnel within their own agencies so that they develop strong and successful career paths that can include foreign postings, to enable successful outcomes for the USG.
6) Relative Advantage of Running a Supporting Mission	The USG is purely an enabler in Colombia. Colombian leaders determine policy objectives and Colombian entities lead operations. This has forced the growth of Colombian capacity and assured HN ownership while allowing a relatively small USG footprint.	6.1 Regularly assess HN capacity and leadership and incorporate findings into U.S. strategic planning. 6.2 Assess expected impact of USG capacity building and reform on HN power structures and assess the threat-level and challenges inherent in retaining a small group of USG entities to provide these capabilities. 6.3 Ensure there is balance in maintaining a small footprint with support and ability to respond to threats or crises such as widespread violence. 6.4 Coordinate niche capabilities, especially among HN LE personnel, especially to maintain or control a situation until better-equipped or specialized forces arrive.

Table 3-2. Summary of Colombia Observations and Recommendations. (cont.)

ENDNOTES - CHAPTER 3

1. The term "Plan Colombia" is commonly used to refer to Colombian and U.S. efforts over an extended period. The initial Plan Colombia ended in 2005 and subsequent extensions and efforts have been known by a variety of terms, including Plan Colombia Phase II, and by the names of component strategies like the Plan Colombia Consolidation Phase, the Colombia Strategic Development Initiative, etc. This study uses "Plan Colombia" to encompass the collection of relevant strategies and initiatives from 2000 onwards.

2. CRS Report for Congress, *Plan Colombia: A Progress Report*, Order Code RL32774, Washington, DC: Congressional Research Service, January 11, 2006, p. 1, available from University of North Texas, *digital.library.unt.edu/govdocs/crs/permalink/meta-crs-8270:1*.

3. *United States Support for Colombia Fact Sheet*, Washington, DC: Department of State, March 28, 2000, available from *www.state.gov/www/regions/wha/colombia/fs_000328_plancolombia.html*.

4. PDD 73 was replaced after 26 months by National Security Policy Directive (NSPD)-18, which also remains classified.

5. Rand Beers, Assistant Secretary for International Narcotics and Law Enforcement Affairs, statement before the Senate Caucus on International Narcotics Control, September 21, 1999, available from Library of Congress Online Catalog, *frwebgate.access.gpo.gov/cgi-bin/getdoc.cgi?dbname=106_house_hearings&docid=f:69868.pdf*.

6. *United States Support for Colombia Fact Sheet*.

7. *Plan Colombia: Drug Reduction Goals Were Not Fully Met, But Security Has Improved; U.S. Agencies Need More Detailed Plans For Reducing Assistance*, (GAO 09-71), Washington, DC: Government Accountability Office, October 2008, pp. 14-15, available from *www.gao.gov/new.items/d0971.pdf*. Also note that the MilGroup manages Foreign Military Financing (FMF), International Military Education and Training (IMET), and Foreign Military Sales

(FMS) programming. These programs, which are funded through the DoS under the Foreign Operations Appropriations Act, are not specific to Colombia, but are provided by the USG to other countries as well.

8. Bureau of International Narcotics and Law Enforcement Affairs, *Counternarcotics and Law Enforcement Country Program: Colombia*, Washington, DC: Department of State, January 2009, available from *www.state.gov/p/inl/rls/fs/113707.htm*.

9. For Social and Economic Justice Programs, funds were increased from $139.7 million to $194.4 million; Rule of Law programs received an increase to $39.4 million from $7.8 million the previous year. Funds for eradication and interdiction were reduced from $591.1 million to $423.4 million. See *Plan Colombia: Drug Reduction Goals Were Not Fully Met, But Security Has Improved*, p. 15.

10. Peter DeShazo, Johanna Mendelson Forman, Phillip McLean, *Countering Threats to Security and Stability in a Failing State: Lessons from Colombia*, Washington, DC: Center for Strategic and International Studies, 2009, p. 18, available from *csis.org/publication/countering-threats-security-and-stability-failing-state*.

11. *Plan Colombia: Drug Reduction Goals Were Not Fully Met, But Security Has Improved*, p. 13.

12. PCCP is also known by other names: "Strategy for Strengthening Democracy and Promoting Social Development" and the "Policy of Consolidation of Democratic Security."

13. *Plan Colombia: Drug Reduction Goals Were Not Fully Met, But Security Has Improved*, pp. 12-13.

14. CSDI is also known by other names: "Strategic Leap," and "National Consolidation Plan."

15. The initial operations in relation to Colombia were mostly conducted by the DEA (between 1976 and 1989). Since then, a large number of USG agencies, including the DEA (which has continued its assistance) are supporting the Colombians.

16. *Plan Colombia: Drug Reduction Goals Were Not Fully Met, But Security Has Improved*, p. 15.

17. This is not to suggest that the USG involvement was planned in this way or even that the USG manages its involvement in Colombia in terms of LOOs. Rather, the LOOs are presented here purely as a (*post facto*) means to understand the continuity and breadth of ways in which LE contributed to achievement of USG objectives in Colombia. See Qualifications and Limitations section on p. 4 for the explanation on how this study formulated the Lines of Operation.

18. *Plan Colombia: Drug Reduction Goals Were Not Fully Met, But Security Has Improved*, pp. 1, 43.

19. The USCG is the lead federal agency for narcotics interdiction.

20. Bureau for International Narcotics and Law Enforcement Affairs, *International Narcotics Control Strategy Report: Volume I, Drug and Chemical Control*, Washington, DC: U.S. Department of State, 2009, p. 205, available from *www.state.gov/p/inl/rls/nrcrpt/2009/index.htm*.

21. *Ibid*., p. 206.

22. With judicial authorization, mobile phones can be tapped anywhere in Colombia.

23. This list, which was introduced during President Clinton's tenure, is used to name and target for sanctions designated nationals and blocked persons.

24. See 21 U.S.C. '1901-1908, 8 U.S.C. '1182, available from *www.treas.gov/offices/enforcement/ofac/programs/narco/drugs.pdf*.

25. "Just the Facts," available from *justf.org/All_Trainees_Country*.

26. *Plan Colombia: A Progress Report*.

CHAPTER 4

KOSOVO

INTRODUCTION

From 1999 to the present, the United States Government (USG) has continuously supported operations on the ground in Kosovo, in addition to a shorter, smaller commitment from October 1998 until the commencement of North Atlantic Treaty Organization (NATO) air operations in March 1999. USG engagement involves a multifaceted commitment that includes Law Enforcement (LE) operations and expertise as part of the comprehensive range of multinational and bilateral, military and civilian missions and programs. The purpose of the LE involvement in these programs and missions has been to support the wider aims and objectives of the respective missions as well as reinforcing the rule of law (RoL) which has been an inherent part of establishing effective governance in the province when it came under international administration after the withdrawal of Yugoslavian security forces from the area in 1999.

The Kosovo example provides valuable insights into the implementation of LE measures in what was a complex operational environment. Part of this complexity results from the duration and the scale of the undertaking. Over the course of more than a decade, the United States and international partners have been involved in the process of establishing security in Kosovo while building effective state institutions (including LE and related ministries and agencies) in a territory that had no recent history of maintaining these institutions. Although the more recent operations in Iraq have exceeded the scale of the Kosovo commitment and have included a large institution building commitment, Kosovo was considered a major commitment at the time and both the United States and the international community still have substantial resources committed in Kosovo.

The international nature of the commitment is an important aspect of the operations in Kosovo. Although the United States has been one of the largest and most consistent contributors of military and civilian resources to Kosovo, most of this commitment has been made through USG contributions to missions run by multinational organizations, principally the United Nations (UN), NATO, the Organization for Security and Cooperation in Europe (OSCE), and the European Union (EU). This has meant that the U.S. involvement has been under the direct leadership of officials from other nations on each of these missions and has been shaped by the need to cooperate with international partners. The differing priorities of international partners has also affected the conduct of these missions with some nations (particularly from Western Europe) having a direct interest in dealing with transnational crime issues in Kosovo, while other nations disagree on Kosovo's status (either as an independent nation or still a province of Yugoslavia).

The USG involvement in LE operations and development programs in Kosovo has also been interagency in nature. The impetus for involvement in Kosovo has been driven by foreign relations imperatives, while relying on expertise from the LE community and on the military to ensure stability and logistic support. This has meant that agencies within the Departments of State, Justice, and Defense have all been involved in planning, funding, conducting, and/or managing operations there. The use of contractors has been the primary means that USG agencies have used to deploy civilian LE expertise in Kosovo; this was one of the earliest operations in which the USG made extensive use of contractors in this manner.[1]

This section investigates the involvement of the USG in the conduct and use of LE to support its strategic objectives in Kosovo. It contains the following material:

- A synopsis of the U.S. operational involvement in Kosovo and LE Lines of Operation
- Observations drawn through research and interviews
- Recommendations drawn through a validation process
- Conclusion

SYNOPSIS (1998-PRESENT)

Unlike the other case studies in this project, Panama and Colombia, the USG had very little direct LE interest in Kosovo, but rather became involved as a part of its wider engagement in the Balkan region. The USG had been involved in the region (including the provision of LE capacity-building expertise) since the commencement of the UN Mission in Bosnia and Herzegovina (UNMIBH) in 1995 and the UN Transitional Authority for Eastern Slavonia (UNTAES) in 1996. While already committed to dealing with other aspects of the breakup of the Yugoslav Federation, the USG did not become involved with Kosovo until 1998. The impetus for involvement came from a desire to end ethnic violence and atrocities in the region, but the primary strategic imperatives driving USG interest were related to stabilizing the region and supporting European security arrangements (such as NATO and the OSCE). The creation of a stable, developing economy and a multi-ethnic democracy in the region was also consistent with the USG's 1989 Support for East European Democracy (SEED) Act. Although these actions would help to reduce the potential for organized crime and terrorism to take root in the area, the direct impact on domestic LE within the United States was not a major consideration.

Yet since committing to operations in Kosovo in 1998, the USG commitment has almost always contained a significant LE component. The initial USG commitment was made as a part of the Kosovo Verification Mission (KVM), an unarmed OSCE-led peace monitoring mission that deployed in October 1998. This mission was to monitor compliance of the Yugoslav security forces and the Kosovo Liberation Army (KLA) with the terms of the Kosovo Verification Agreement of October 12, 1998. Given the need to monitor Yugoslav Ministry of Interior forces, the KVM included international police observers (including from the United States) as a part of its contingent. However, the KVM was unable to prevent another outbreak of fighting in December 1998. The KVM monitors were eventually withdrawn in March 1999. The next phase in USG commitment to Kosovo was leadership of Operation ALLIED FORCE, the NATO air campaign against Serbia and Yugoslav forces in Kosovo to force a Yugoslavian withdrawal from the province and acceptance of the Rambouillet Accords. This air campaign was conducted between March 22 and June 11, 1999, and marked the only period of U.S. operational commitment that did not have an LE component.

The success of Operation ALLIED FORCE set the conditions for the entry of NATO forces, designated as the Kosovo Force (KFOR) to oversee the withdrawal of Yugoslav army and police forces and to accept responsibility for security in the province. The Yugoslav withdrawal (in accordance with the Rambouillet agreement) also required the international community to take responsibility for transitional authority in Kosovo and the international presence was authorized under UN Security Council Resolution (UNSCR) 1244 on June 10, 1999. In addition to the existence of separate military and civilian components of the international response, the civilian responsibilities were further complicated by the involvement of several multinational organizations in its composition. Initially, the OSCE was expected to take the lead on the mission and had developed much of the planning for civil governance and capacity building. However, in an 11th-hour agreement, all civilian multinational involvement was to be brought under the overall coordination of the UN Interim Administration Mission in Kosovo (UNMIK), with specific responsibilities for different areas (known as "Pillars") allocated among the multinational organizations as follows:

- Pillar I: Initially, Humanitarian Assistance (led by the UN High Commissioner for Refugees), but was redesignated as Police and Justice (UN-led) after June 2000
- Pillar II: Civil Administration (UN-led)
- Pillar III: Democratization and Institution Building (led by the OSCE)
- Pillar IV: Reconstruction and Economic Development (EU-led)

See Figure 4-1.

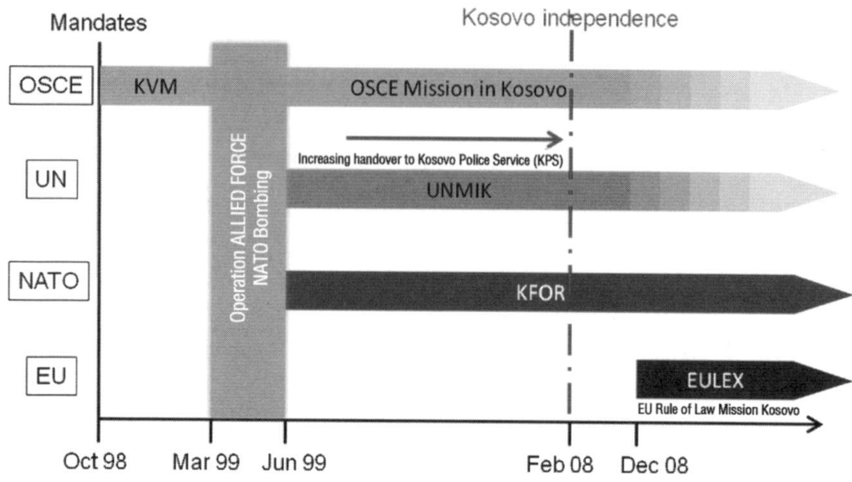

Figure 4-1. Timeline of the Various Multinational Missions in Kosovo.

The United States did not provide the leadership of KFOR (initially led by British General Sir Michael Jackson), UNMIK (the initial Special Representative for the Secretary-General [SRSG] was French Diplomat Bernard Kouchner), nor for any of the four pillars, but was and remained a major contributor to the success of the international commitment throughout this period. The United States provided leadership of and the main component of one of KFOR's five Multinational Task Forces, as well as the largest contingent of police officers (not including Formed Police Units) in the UNMIK and the leadership of the OSCE police training mission.

The United States has maintained continuous support to Kosovo even beyond the nation's declaration of independence on February 17, 2008. However, Kosovo's independence was accompanied by substantial changes in the way this support has been provided.

On the one hand, it has seen the commencement (on December 1, 2009) of the EU Rule of Law Mission in Kosovo (EULEX) as the primary multinational monitoring, mentoring, and assistance (MMA) mission in Kosovo, focusing on support to Kosovo's police, judges, and prosecutors, and inheriting many of the responsibilities of the UNMIK and the OSCE Mission. Although not a member of the EU, the United States is a contributing partner in the EULEX (along with four non-EU nations). However, due to opposition from member states (including Turkey within NATO, Spain within the EU, Russia in the OSCE, and both Russia and China in the UN) none of the four multinational organizations with missions in Kosovo (NATO, EU, OSCE, and UN) have recognized Kosovo's independence, instead they have maintained a "status neutral" position which effectively accepts that Kosovo is still a part of Serbia. This has complicated the ability of the main donor states (including the United States and Germany) to pursue a long-term development strategy for law enforcement in Kosovo. Hence, while still retaining a major commitment to both NATO and the EULEX, the USG also provides important capacity-building assistance programs to Kosovo on a bilateral basis.

Overall, the U.S. involvement in Kosovo, particularly in support of developing law enforcement capacity, has been successful. As a result of the efforts of the multinational missions (all of which have had substantial U.S. involvement) and of the bilateral assistance (of which the United States has been the largest donor), Kosovo has been relatively stable and developing to the point where, with (albeit incomplete) international recognition, the province was able to declare its independence in 2008. In particular, the development of the Kosovo Police Service (KPS), established from scratch since 1999 and formally known as the Kosovo Police since 2008, has been a substantial achievement in which (despite some shortcomings in senior leadership and specialized investigative capabilities) the service is highly regarded by the population, has the lowest reported levels of corruption in the Balkans, and has maintained an ethnic balance that approximates that of the wider population.

Even though the U.S. commitment was not motivated by law enforcement priorities, law enforcement operations and capacity building have been, and continue to be, an important component of the U.S. contribution to the Kosovo intervention. The enforcement of law and the maintenance of order have been important in the establishment of a safe and secure environment. Also, supporting the development of RoL in Kosovo is a vital part of achieving the wider objectives of the international mission in that country.

LINES OF OPERATION

Given the length of the U.S. involvement in Kosovo, the involvement of such a variety of agencies and multinational missions with different agendas, and the major phases that the international intervention has progressed through, it is useful to consider the USG involvement in terms of a number of distinct, but interrelated lines of operation (LOOs).[2] This section describes the three major LOOs identified:

1. Deployed Law Enforcement Operations, Observers and Advisers,
2. Capacity-building of Kosovo Ministries and Agencies, and
3. Military (KFOR) Operations.

See Table 4-1.

LOO 1 **Deployed Law Enforcement Operations, Observers and Advisers**	1a. Observer Mission 1b. Interim Law Enforcement and MMA 1c. Post-Independence MMA and Continued Executive Mandate
LOO 2 **Capacity-building of Kosovo Ministries and Agencies**	2a. Multilateral Programs 2b. Bilateral Programs
LOO 3 **Military (KFOR) Operations**	3a. Legal Reform, Mentoring and Advising 3b. Employment of General Purpose Forces

Table 4-1. Summary of Lines of Operation (LOO) for Kosovo.

LOO 1—DEPLOYED LAW ENFORCEMENT OPERATIONS, OBSERVERS, AND ADVISERS.

The most direct involvement of law enforcement in a mission is by the deployment of civilian law enforcement professionals for operational tasks. During the course of U.S. involvement in Kosovo, this activity has had three main phases: deployment of police observers as a part of the OSCE-led KVM; the U.S. contribution to the civilian police component of the UNMIK (with Executive Authority for law enforcement); and the employment of U.S. civilian police (in both the UNMIK and the subsequent EULEX mission) for MMA of the fledging KPS.

Observer Mission.

The KVM was the short-lived OSCE-led mission that deployed to Kosovo in October 1998 to monitor adherence to the Kosovo Verification Agreement by the Kosovo Liberation Army and the Yugoslavian security forces. Although this was a primarily military mission, the need to monitor the activity of Yugoslav police forces (who had played an important role in the campaign to suppress the Kosovo independence movement prior to international intervention) meant that there was the requirement for police expertise among the 2,000 verifiers authorized.

The police contingent among the KVM was small and largely staffed by European police. Even though many of these officers returned to Kosovo after the NATO bombing to work with the UNMIK or OSCE Mission, their relatively small numbers did not have a large impact on the follow-on missions. Precise details of numbers and activities of U.S. involvement in the KVM are not available, but the main impact of the KVM was to get the international LE focused agencies of the Department of State (DoS) and Department of Justice (DoJ) involved in initial planning for a potential follow-on commitment in Kosovo. The USG support to the KVM was managed by the Department of Justice's International Criminal Investigative Training Assistance Program (ICITAP). In addition to its monitoring task, this USG element was also tasked to investigate options for establishing police training centers under the assumption that a follow-on mission was likely.

Interim Law Enforcement and MMA.

This line of operation refers to U.S. support for the multinational missions in Kosovo that had responsibility for enforcing law under the executive mandate and for MMA of the KPS. This was accomplished by deployment of contracted American police officers to serve with the UNMIK and continued (albeit on an incrementally reduced scale of direct operational activity) until the U.S.-recognized declaration of independence by Kosovo in February 2008.

UNSCR 1244 was one of few occasions where the UN Security Council has authorized Executive Authority for an armed police mission. This unprecedented decision by the UN was largely due to U.S. initiative in proposing it and developing a concept of operations that helped overcome initial reluctance by European powers. This made the UNMIK responsible for all aspects of governance in Kosovo and gave the international community great latitude in its decision-making and authority to effect its objectives.

However, the extent of the responsibilities implicit in this mandate created numerous problems for the international commitment. One problem was in bringing sufficient numbers of officers with a range of capabilities from UN member states into Kosovo in an appropriate timeframe. The UN International Civilian Police (UNPOL) was to be the LE authority in the province and was expected to be in position in sufficient numbers to take over internal security responsibilities from the KFOR within 3 months after the initial military deployment. However, the UNPOL did not have sufficient capability to deploy into many parts of Kosovo until early 2000 and did not reach its peak strength of over 3,300 officers (from more than 50 nations) until 2001.[3] Part of the delay was due to the late decision to make the UN responsible for international police commitment (rather than the OSCE, which had done most of the preparations for the role). The UN made this decision shortly before issuing UNSCR 1244, so the UN had not invested much time in preliminary planning for the task before the commencement of the operation. Also difficult was the need to identify (from the various UN member states) and deploy sufficient numbers of personnel across the full range of LE capabilities necessary to maintain this comprehensive responsibility. This included the need for specialist roles such as border control, judicial protection[4] and prisoner transportation. Drawing on police from such a wide variety of nations also created discrepancies in the quality, capabilities and approach to law enforcement of the personnel deployed. As with the commitments to the KFOR, caveats imposed by contributing nations provided further limitations on coordination.

The creation and deployment of Stability Police Units (SPUs)[5] was a particular development of interest in the UNMIK. The inclusion of SPUs in the UNMIK was envisaged to provide the UNPOL with formed bodies of police to fulfill riot control and high-risk policing functions to relieve the reliance on military forces in order maintenance functions. The first SPU did not deploy until April 2000, and, given shortcomings in the capability of these units and the deployment by NATO of Multinational Specialized Units (MSUs)[6], SPUs were often used in more static facility and protective security roles rather than on riot control tasks.[7] Hence, the efficacy of civilian policing on the operation was often dependent upon the availability of the KFOR back-up (including MSUs) in periods of escalating tension,[8] even after the deployment of SPUs.

The United States was the largest contributor of police personnel to the UNMIK mission. At its peak, the United States had 605 officers (all as individually-deployed personnel; the United States did not provide an SPU) in Kosovo. All personnel were recruited (mostly from a variety of U.S. state and local agencies), trained and administered by a contracting company for 12-month deployments to the UNMIK. Using this means, the United States was able to provide a well-regarded, well-equipped contingent of police officers to the mission. However, recruitment of police professionals by contractors draws from a relatively small pool of qualified and available personnel, so there were a few cases of less than suitable personnel (unfit or inappropriately qualified) deployed with the contingents. Another recruitment problem was attracting the right range of law enforcement personnel; although salaries offered by the contractor were very competitive for generalist officers from smaller departments, they were less attractive to still-active personnel from big city departments or officers with management or specialist expertise. Use of a contracting company as an intermediary also created difficulties in dismissing and disciplining officers, and still required government involvement in, and close supervision of, the predeployment training provided in order to ensure the required standards were maintained. In addition, this did not provide a way to institutionalize knowledge and provide for long-term capacity.

Several offices from two bureaus within the DoS were mostly responsible for managing this program. Policy oversight for Kosovo and communication with the U.S. diplomatic mission was by the Office of South Central European Affairs (EUR/SCE). The Office of Regional Political-Military Affairs (EUR/RPM) was responsible for coordinating with the EU and OSCE. Another office in the Europe bureau, the Office of the Assistance Coordinator for Europe and Eurasia (EUR/ACE), was responsible for allocating SEED Act funding to the State-run programs. The Bureau for International Narcotics and Law Enforcement Affairs (INL) provided advice on law enforcement matters and managed the support to the UNMIK UNPOL via its Office of Civilian Police and Rule of Law (INL/CIV). The Bureau of Political-Military Affairs played a coordinating function and, under National Security Council (NSC) guidance, chaired the Inter-Agency Working Group on Kosovo which was first convened in early 1999. This Working Group brought together representatives (at the Assistant Secretary or Deputy Assistant Secretary level) from the NSC, the DoS, the Department of Defense (DoD), and the DoJ to manage the USG response to the developing crisis. At the higher level, this working group contributed to the development (under the direction of the DoS Special Advisor for the Balkans) of the Political-Military Plan. At the height of the Kosovo crisis (during the NATO bombing campaign and initial deployment of the KFOR and UNMIK), this Working Group met daily or at least every other day.

From the perspective of developing a plan for USG law enforcement support to the UN mission, this working group worked well. This was aided by the significant, firm, and long-term commitment and policy guidance on Kosovo from the USG leadership at that time. Further, due to the experience of previous missions in Haiti, Bosnia, and Eastern Slovenia, the personnel in the various agencies already had high degrees of familiarity with each other and the likely LE issues that could arise. As a reflection of this, the INL had drafted a concept of operations for LE in the province which became the LE annex to the Rambouillet Agreement; this was rejected by the Serbs, but served as the basis for USG shaping of OSCE and UN planning for LE in Kosovo and was the genesis of the proposal for international armed police with Executive Authority. However, due to the separate

planning for the KFOR conducted by the DoD (which was outside DoS channels of coordination), the INL was unable to have civilian policing and deployment issues included in the KFOR planning. As the situation in Kosovo stabilized and operations reached a steady state, coordination for Kosovo was eventually delegated to working level desk officers, primarily within the DoS, the DoD, and the NSC, for routine conferences and the ability to refer decisions via the hierarchy of less-regular Initial Planning Conferences, Deputies Committees, Principals Committee, and the NSC as required.

Although the police officers who were the U.S. contribution to the UNPOL were formally working under UNMIK direction, the DoS had a mechanism to provide in-country oversight of the deployed U.S. police contingent through a deployed INL Police Advisor. The Police Advisor was a USG employee who reported directly to the INL about both the UNPOL commitment and initially the capacity building support to the OSCE (see LOO 2a). This position also fulfilled an important communication link between the operational deployment and the USG Head of Mission. By 2003, the U.S. contingent was also filling the position of Deputy Commissioner for Operations in the UNPOL hierarchy.

Within Kosovo, many of the relationships between the UNMIK police and the other various elements of the international presence were built primarily on interpersonal relationships and the initiative of individuals involved. Given the division of responsibilities for executive authority, policing, and LE capacity building, the cooperation between the UNMIK and the OSCE mission on issues of recruitment and selection (an OSCE responsibility) and mentoring trained

junior HN police (an UNMIK responsibility) was very important. The close relationship between the first UNMIK police commissioner and the American head of the Kosovo Police Service School (KPSS, see LOO 2a) resulted in an arrangement in which senior UNPOL personnel were consulted in the recruitment of Kosovo police, and the OSCE provided training at the KPSS for UNPOL Field Training Officers (FTOs) to better them for the MMA role. The UNPOL link to the KFOR was particularly important given the mutual reliance on each other in the conduct of security tasks and this required not only cooperation at the national level, but also coordination at the local level. At the highest level, the closeness of this relationship fluctuated over the course of time based on the personalities of the respective UNPOL Commissioners and KFOR Commanders. These missions exchanged liaison officers and held regular meetings, but had no unified command or standing arrangements for integrated planning to mitigate the effects of personality. At the lowest level (station-level), UNPOL-KFOR relations were also personality-driven and in the American-led KFOR sector (Multi-National Task Force-East [MNTF-E]), American military personnel found that this cooperation could be better facilitated when they had American (or German, United Kingdom [UK] or other Western national) UNPOL officers assigned to their districts. In some cases early in the deployment, the quality of these relationships led to the establishment of stations staffed jointly by KFOR and UNPOL personnel.

Post-Independence MMA and Continued Executive Mandate.

This line of operation is the continuation of LOO 1b beyond the declaration of independence by Kosovo in February 2008. By this stage, the UNMIK had already handed over most LE responsibilities to the KPS (known as the KP since independence) by the end of 2004 so the operational capabilities of the UNPOL had already been drawn down to that of a primarily MMA commitment. However this stage was different largely because of the complicated circumstances of Kosovo independence which was not recognized by the UN. Hence the UNMIK still formally retained the executive authority granted under UNSCR 1244.[9]

Another major feature of this LOO was the commencement of the EU-led EULEX mission in December 2008. The EULEX has a much narrower mandate than the UNMIK. It has concentrated on support to the RoL system and has three main components: Police (initially the EULEX had 400 international personnel in MMA roles and several hundred in executive roles), Justice (100 personnel), and Customs (approximately 25 personnel). The EULEX has also inherited the residual UNSCR 1244 Executive Authority from the UNMIK and has an Executive Department which operates in three areas. First, the EULEX still provides the policing authority (including command over KP personnel) in several enclaves in the north and over two check points on the border with Serbia. Second, the international police presence maintains a Rapid Reaction Force (with Special Weapons and Tactics [SWAT] and riot control capabilities) to provide back-up to the KP when required. Finally, EULEX police retain capabilities for investigation and intelligence, particularly related to war crimes, trafficking, and organized crime. MMA personnel have no authority over their KP counterparts and cannot intervene in KP actions, even when then may be counterproductive. Many of the EULEX police personnel are former UNPOL personnel (from EU and partner nations) who remained in Kosovo and transferred to the EULEX.

The United States is a major contributor to the EULEX, with personnel assigned to both the Police and Justice areas. Support to the latter consists of up to four prosecutors or judges provided by the DoS (EUR/ACE). The commitment of police is much more substantial with 80 U.S. personnel deployed (as of August 2009) of which 60 percent were in MMA roles, most of the remainder in the Executive and a small commitment of police to the Justice area (for prisoner transportation, etc). The United States provides key leadership positions in the EULEX, including the Head of the Executive Department (one of the Deputy Commissioners) and the Deputy Head of the Organized Crime Investigation Unit.

The USG management of this LOO is a direct continuation of LOO 1b. A desk officer within the DoS (INL/CIV) provides the oversight from Washington and coordinates with other agencies within the Department. In Kosovo, the INL/CIV is represented by an In-Country Contract Officer Representative (ICOR, a USG employee), who deals directly with the contracting company and their office in Pristina. The ICOR is located in the Embassy and also reports to the Ambassador on issues related to the EULEX commitment as well as acting as an advisor on law enforcement issues (the Federal Bureau of Investigation [FBI] has no representative in Kosovo because criminal activities in Kosovo are judged to have little direct effect on the U.S. domestic law enforcement situation).

LOO 2—CAPACITY-BUILDING OF KOSOVO MINISTRIES AND AGENCIES.

The components of this line of operation involve capacity building support to Kosovo law enforcement and related institutions. Capacity building includes formal training, recruitment, capability development, administrative assistance, provision of materiel, and other support required to build new capabilities or agencies or to expand the size of existing capabilities. This is to be distinguished from MMA, which works to assist and observe existing capabilities or capabilities that are being developed by the host nation (HN) or a third party.

A priority for capacity building for both the United States and the multinational missions in Kosovo has been to create a multi-ethnic, effective police service (and associated institutions) that operate in accordance with democratic governance principles. No indigenous Kosovo police service or supporting ministry and judicial and corrections system existed in the province when the multinational missions started in 1999. The United States has been a major contributor to the development of these institutions, both in its support of the multinational missions and through direct support to the Kosovo government.

Multilateral Programs.

This line of operation involves the USG in the law enforcement capacity building components of the multinational missions in Kosovo. This support commenced in 1999 and had concluded by 2008 with the withdrawal of OSCE support to the KPSS.

At the commencement of the UNMIK mission in 1999, the OSCE had responsibility for "Democratization and Institution Building" as Pillar III of the mission. (The OSCE provided one of the four Deputy Special Representatives to the Secretary-General [DSRSG] to lead this pillar within the wider UNMIK structure). As a part of this role, the OSCE mission was responsible for establishing the institutions for maintenance of rule of law in the province, including the creation of the KPS.

The main element of the U.S. commitment to the OSCE mission was in the development of the KPS. From the outset of the mission, the ICITAP seconded to the OSCE a senior police manager to fill the position of Director of Police Development and Education (working directly under the DSRSG) and has also since contributed several hundred instructors (mostly U.S. or host nation contractors, but also including several USG employees) over the course of the commitment.[10] This commitment commenced in Kosovo in early July 1999 (within 2 weeks after the cessation of the NATO air campaign) and immediately focused on the priorities of recruitment and the establishment of the KPSS. With a staff of 12 international personnel, including several who were part of the KVM deployment, the Police Development and Education element of the OSCE Mission was able to commence training the first class of KPS officers on September 7, 1999. In order to achieve this, the staff needed to coordinate with the KFOR for security, transportation and the allocation of a site in Vushtrri[11] for the school and with the UNPOL for KPS recruiting and initial planning for KPS mentoring and employment. There were no formal procedures governing this coordination in the initial stages, rather precedents and protocols were established effectively due to the unity of effort and cooperative nature of relationships between individuals in each organization.

The training of the KPS faced manifold problems at these early stages. The creation of a multiethnic, effective, democratic service was complicated by a very fragmented post-war society as well as by the legacy of Yugoslavian governance in which police were seen to serve the state rather than to protect the population. The students were also products of a Communist-era education system based on rote learning, which also made teaching concepts difficult. As an OSCE Mission, the international instructors were provided mainly from developed Western European and North American nations and thus not marked by the great differences in the quality of personnel experienced by the UNPOL. Yet even among these nations, there were substantial differences in the approaches to and organization of policing, and the conditions under which it is conducted which was reflected in some inconsistencies and contradictions in the training provided. There were also disagreements over the appropriate length of training for KPS officers. These divergent views also existed among the U.S. agencies involved, with the DoS advocating for a 6-week course (to grow numbers quickly) and the DoJ supporting a 6-month program (as the ideal length of training). The compromise made was for an initial 5-week basic course, followed by 7 weeks of advanced training, which was incrementally delivered in rotation between the field and the KPSS, as well as a structured FTO Program. In later courses, 20 weeks became the standard.

The training of the KPS is now considered one of the greatest successes of the Kosovo intervention. The KPS was one of the first institutions to transition to

HN control, is one of the most respected Kosovo institutions among the population, and has the lowest reported corruption levels compared with other police forces in the region. The Community Policing program was one of the legacy achievements in the training provided to the KPS. Community Police, coupled with competent police development, was a pioneering program and one emulated throughout the region, which accounts for the trust and confidence the people have in "their" police.

The OSCE handed over control of the school to HN control in 2006. It was renamed the Kosovo Center for Public Safety Education and Development (KCPSED) and also became responsible for training emergency services, customs and corrections personnel. The last U.S. personnel assigned to the KCPSED were withdrawn by 2008.

Within the USG, the personnel and technical expertise to manage this LOO was provided by the ICITAP. However, the funding and policy direction for the ICITAP's involvement were provided via the INL's Office of Asia, Africa and Europe Programs (INL/AAE) and allocated and managed above that level by the same mechanisms as for LOO 1b. However in the initial stages of the operation, due to the instability of the situation on the ground and their status as a secondment to the OSCE, the senior ICITAP manager on the ground had a great degree of latitude for action with little direct involvement by U.S.-based agencies.

Bilateral Programs.

This line of operation refers to capacity building support to law enforcement and related institutions by USG agencies provided directly to the Kosovo

Government ministries and agencies. The number of programs supporting this LOO has increased since 2004, and the LOO continues to the present time. All capacity building support to Kosovo from the USG is now provided via bilateral programs.

Although USG agencies had commenced bilateral programs prior to 2008, in the post-independence period they have become the only mechanisms by which the USG provides capacity building support to Kosovo. Furthermore, the United States is recognized as not only the largest provider of capacity-building support to Kosovo, but also the only nation to have been consistently involved in these efforts (both multinational and bilateral) since 1999. The range of U.S. agencies involved in capacity building in post-independence Kosovo also reveals the breadth of engagement necessary for various aspects of LE to work effectively within a functioning RoL system.

The DoJ has two agencies committed in Kosovo. The ICITAP has maintained a continuous presence in the country since its initial involvement in the OSCE Mission (see LOO 2a), but has become increasingly involved in bilateral programs in support of the KPS (later Kosovo Police [KP]) as well as support to the Ministry of Internal Affairs (MOIA) which oversees the KP. The ICITAP currently has five Program Activities in Kosovo: MOIA Assistance which includes assistance in drafting legislation and policies relevant to law enforcement; Border Security and Immigration Control; Trafficking in Persons; Policing Across Ethnic Boundaries; and Integrated Data Management. Previous specific achievements under ICITAP bilateral programs include the establishment and building of the Central Kosovo Police Forensic Laboratory. These reflect the current capabilities and needs for the KP in that basic policing skills are no longer a development priority, but the needs are now for management of the force, specialist policing skills and reinforcing the multiethnic nature of the service. It also reflects a greater focus on institution-building rather than individual training. To run these programs, the ICITAP has one direct hire USG employee and seven U.S. contractors in Kosovo, with all other staff being locally employed. The other DoJ presence is from the Office of Overseas Prosecutorial Development, Assistance, and Training (OPDAT). Like the ICITAP, the OPDAT has been involved in Kosovo since 1999 and has maintained between one and three Resident Legal Advisors (RLAs) in the country. The OPDAT's focus is on assisting with the development of the Kosovo criminal justice system, including legislation (criminal codes and procedural codes) and training for prosecutors and judges. Most of this work has been conducted on a bilateral basis since 1999, but coordinated with OSCE, UNMIK, and other multinational programs. The poor cooperation between investigators and prosecutors in Kosovo is an important problem; hence efforts in these areas have a direct effect on law enforcement. Furthermore, the ICITAP and OPDAT programs coordinate their efforts (including the conduct of joint training), particularly in initiatives targeting the trafficking of persons and narcotics. Both ICITAP and OPDAT programs are run in accordance with the Embassy's Mission Strategic Plan (MSP) and the in-country representatives of each agency contribute to the development of that plan. Both agencies report back to their respective DoJ agencies for technical and administrative support, but are funded by SEED funding via the INL. Unlike LOO 1c, this is managed by the INL/AAE, rather than the INL/CIV. Since August 2009, the INL/AAE has had a representative in the Kosovo Embassy to oversee the ICITAP and OPDAT programs.

Other agencies manage capacity-building programs that, although not involved directly in law enforcement, contribute to the effectiveness of host nation law enforcement. The U.S. Agency for International Development (USAID) is not permitted to be involved in building police or criminal justice capacity, but runs programs in Kosovo aimed at building effectiveness of the wider RoL system. Current major programs are: the Justice Support Program which builds the institutional effectiveness of the court system (including administration, improving public access to the justice system and professionalization of judges and other court staff); the Lawyer Development Program with training for lawyers (not including criminal prosecutors) and developing the local bar association; and Anti-Trafficking in Persons which concentrates on prevention, public awareness and prosecution by working with at risk communities. The DoS's Bureau of International Security and Nonproliferation (ISN) also maintains a presence in Kosovo as a part of its Export Control and Related Border Security (EXBS) program. The EXBS is specifically focused on restricting the proliferation of weapons of mass destruction and dual-use technologies. However, this is achieved by building host nation capacity (including the provision of specialist equipment developed in cooperation with the Defense Threat Reduction Agency) for border control including the KP border division and the Customs Service, thereby contributing directly to law enforcement effectiveness in border security. The EXBS receives its funding directly from the ISN rather than from SEED funding and although their representative consults in development of the MSP, the EXBS does not justify its Kosovo funding via the MSP.

The DoD also has the ability to support training of host nation security forces. Under the International Military Education and Training (IMET) program, the U.S. Defense Attaché (DATT) is able to fund training of Kosovo personnel; this has primarily been used to send officers for specialist training (such as counterterrorism) at the Marshall Center. Although the Kosovo Security Force (KSF) is the primary recipient of Defense assistance, IMET funds can be used for training of personnel from any of the security forces, including the KP and Customs Service.

LOO 3—MILITARY (KFOR) OPERATIONS

Although the U.S. military role was not specifically focused on enforcing law, experience in Kosovo (and other recent operations) has seen an increasing convergence of military and LE responsibilities, operations, and areas of interest. This has been due to both the applicability of specific military capabilities to support LE activity and the fact that early in the operation the KFOR was the only element of the operation with sufficient capability and capacity to maintain law and order across Kosovo.

Employment of Military Police in Legal Reform, Mentoring, and Advising.

U.S. Army Military Police (MP) have played a prominent role in law enforcement (both military and civilian) as a part of the international commitment in Kosovo. Although the size, role and extent of the MP commitment have declined since 1999, the U.S. Army has maintained an MP presence in Kosovo until the present time.

The first MP presence in Kosovo was an MP Task Force (designated as TF 793[12]) which deployed as a part of the MNTF-E (see LOO 3b). The TF was a composite MP battalion, consisting of three MP companies (from different battalions) reinforced by military working dog teams and 10 Special Agents from Criminal Investigation Command (CID).

On the initial occupation of Kosovo, TF 793 was tasked to support the MNTF-E in the traditional MP roles of battlefield circulation (i.e. military traffic control), area security and prisoner of war operations, but with additional specific tasks to occupy and operate the border control point from Macedonia, assist in the occupation of the two largest towns in the MNTF-E sector (Ferizaj and Gjilan) and to occupy the police stations. The role for the MPs quickly evolved into four main functions: deterring looting and other crime; running detention facilities; running the police stations; and facilitating the return of refugees (who started to cross back into Kosovo within a month of the KFOR's arrival). Although the requirement for a border security task was identified prior to deployment, the complexity of dealing with the role (including checkpoint control, immigration, and customs) which fell to the MPs was not adequately accounted for in pre-deployment planning. Border security and battlefield circulation issues were exacerbated by the lack of a UN plan to deal with refugees, who returned to Kosovo earlier and in greater numbers than expected. The MPs maintained substantial responsibility for law and order within the MNTF-E sector during the first years of the KFOR commitment. Predeployment planning had assumed that this would be required until the arrival of sufficient international civilian personnel, but the UNPOL did not take over executive authority in the sector until early 2000. The MPs, by virtue of their domestic garrison law enforcement role, did have some experience in these duties, but were a small force which limited their capacity to deal with crime in the community. The size and limited authority of the CID element imposed further restrictions. Furthermore, effective Executive Authority also relied on an RoL system that was under-developed, meaning that MP commanders had to deal with issues related to the applicability of various versions of the local criminal code. The military detention system was primarily trained for prisoner of war handling, and although able to detain persons of security concern this was a short-term expedient that had to suffice until the civilian criminal justice system was rehabilitated.

Handling civil disturbances was another important role for the MPs before the establishment of effective UNPOL capability in the U.S. sector. Although riot control is a core MP competency, the scale and intensity of disturbances in early 2000 had not been anticipated. Even after the UNPOL assumption of executive authority, the MPs continued to be involved in this role as they offered a more robust riot control capability than the UNPOL in the sector.

The MPs needed to work closely with the UNPOL even after the latter established presence at stations in the sector. However, the process for coordination between the civilian and military police had not been articulated in advance, so these systems were developed on the basis of local initiative and hence the extent and quality of cooperation varied. The closest working relationships were developed with UNPOL officers and leadership from the U.S. and other nations, such as Germany and the U.K., that have similar policing approaches and standards. During the early period of the KFOR commitment (at least until late 2001), in some areas the MPs would man stations jointly with UNPOL and KPS officers, with MPs providing security for the station, ability to reinforce UNPOL/KPS, and a liaison conduit to the KFOR. The MPs had no formal role in training KPS personnel, but did on occasion provide assistance to collocated UNPOL personnel in their advisory role, as well as providing ad hoc mentoring to collocated KP personnel.

Since 2002, the scope of MP responsibilities and the size of the commitment have been drawn down. In line with the rest of U.S. KFOR, the MP contingent has been largely staffed by National Guard personnel. The current U.S. MP commitment to the MNTF-E consists of the Provost Marshal Office (PMO) which has LE and security responsibilities for Camp Bondsteel and MNTF-E personnel. The MNTF-E also has a Joint Law Enforcement Liaison Team (JLELT) which conducts liaison with the KP in their sector, and one CID agent.

Throughout the period of U.S. commitment, the MP contingent has remained under the direct command of the U.S.-led component of the KFOR (MNTF-E). However, they do also have reporting responsibilities to the KFOR Provost Marshal.

Employment of General Purpose Forces.

This line of operation describes the use of non-MP U.S. military forces in roles that supported the establishment and maintenance of law and order in Kosovo. This commenced in 1999 with the initial KFOR deployment and continues to the present time. The peak strength of U.S. military forces in the KFOR was 7,000 and is currently approximately 1,400.

The U.S. military has remained a major contributor to the KFOR since the mission's inception and has retained leadership of one of the five subordinate formations (MNTF-E) within the KFOR for that entire period. Task Force Falcon (as the U.S. contingent within MNTF-E was initially called) was a brigade sized force consisting of three maneuver battalions and an MP battalion. MNTF-E Headquarters also had command over a Polish/Ukrainian battalion and a Greek battalion and tactical control over a Russian airborne brigade and an attack helicopter unit from the United Arab Emirates (UAE).

MNTF-E entered Kosovo on June 12, 1999, and among its tasks was "ensuring public safety and order until the international civilian presence can take responsibility for this task."[13] As discussed in LOOs 1b and 3a, the UNPOL was not in a position to accept this responsibility in this sector until early 2000, effectively leaving the KFOR with Executive Authority for this period. Although the MP battalion had primary responsibility for explicit law and order tasks, due to their presence patrolling across the sector, the non-MP components of MNTF-E work involved, in part, responding to security and crime concerns of the population. Even when the UNPOL had a more effective presence, the MNTF-E continued to run presence operations and to detain criminals, often without coordination with the UNPOL. When liaison did occur, it was the result of the strength of working relationships between proactive officers. Following the reduction of the strength of the KFOR after 2002, U.S. KFOR personnel have played a less direct, active role in population security. Presence patrols are much less frequent and U.S. forces will only intervene *in extremis.*

Due to the security mandate of the KFOR, U.S. forces in Kosovo have had responsibilities as a part of the response to civil disturbances. Prior to the arrival of the UNPOL and the establishment of the KPS, the KFOR was the only agency able to respond to riots. Even though the main element within the MNTF-E for conducting this role was the MP Task Force (LOO 3a), the general purpose elements contributed to these operations by controlling approaches to the scene of unrest, command and control, assistance in removing obstacles, and providing a final line of security in case the MPs became hard-pressed. At the theater-level, the KFOR also had the MSU (a unit consisting of personnel from European *gendarmerie* forces) specifically to deal with these types of incidents. However, the MSU elements were usually deployed in higher threat sectors of Kosovo, such as Pristina and in the north. When they did operate together, U.S. forces generally had good working relationships with and respect for the MSUs, but difficulties identified were a lack of understanding of the MSU capability by some subordinate commanders, different rules of engagement (RoE), and language differences.[14] The international response to a series of riots in 2004 was marked by confusion about the respective roles of and coordination between KFOR elements, the MSU, UNPOL's SPUs, and the KPS. Since that time, protocols have established a three-tiered response to a major security event with the KP as the first responders, the UNPOL (later EULEX) to provide first level of back-up, and the KFOR to intervene only if the police response is likely to be overwhelmed. A formal request needs to be made between the top leadership of each agency before the next tier of support can be provided. However, KFOR elements can pre-position in anticipation of the possible need for such support and can provide outer cordon security (in cooperation with the police) prior to any formal request.

Border security, combating organized crime and explosive ordnance disposal (EOD) are other areas in which U.S. KFOR elements and law enforcement agencies share interests. The conduct of "border monitoring duties" was a specific responsibility of the KFOR at the commencement of the operation.[15] The security and operation of border checkpoints is no longer managed by the KFOR, but the patrolling of the international borders remains a KFOR task until 2011 when the KP will assume this responsibility (except for the Administrative Boundary Line between Serbia and Kosovo, which will remain a KFOR task). The KFOR is currently mentoring KP border police during the conduct of joint border patrol operations. In the conduct of their "safe and secure environment" mission, the KFOR was specifically interested in preventing the flow of weapons into Kosovo and also the potential for weapons being smuggled out into neighboring Macedonia. This concerned border security as well as driving the KFOR's interest in eradicating organized crime. The U.S. military had substantial intelligence assets that could contribute to the counter organized crime task, but issues with sharing classified material prevented full participation in the UNPOL's organized crime task force. Finally, despite the KP having EOD units, as late as 2009 the KP have no element stationed in the MNTF-E sector, hence the U.S. Army EOD capability has the task as primary responder to all EOD incidents there.

The MNTF-E is under the command of Headquarters KFOR, which is a multinational headquarters staffed by NATO nations. Command of the KFOR has not been held by a U.S. officer; however the U.S. Army has provided officers to fill senior staff appointments (such as Deputy Chief of Staff for Operations and Intelligence) among the rotation of U.S. personnel since 1999. The KFOR is a NATO operation and comes under command of the Supreme Allied Commander Europe, via the subordinate command of Allied Joint Force Command Naples. The United States has a DATT in the Embassy at Pristina, however this officer has reporting channels to the U.S. European Command and to the Ambassador and has no command relationship with the KFOR or with the U.S. elements of the KFOR.

OBSERVATIONS AND RECOMMENDATIONS

The observations from the research and workshop on Kosovo were grouped into six main thematic areas: (1) Control and Coordination, (2) Executive Authority, (3) Use of Contractors, (4) Military Role, (5) Organized Crime, and (6) Border Security. In this section, a series of recommendations follows each observation.

1. Control and Coordination.

Numerous USG agencies were involved in interdependent parts of the mission, with disparate funding lines and strategic oversight. In-country coordination and planning between the USG and international partners often relied on informal and ad-hoc personal relationships and mutual willingness to cooperate.

Most of the USG funding for the Kosovo mission was channeled through the DoD and DoS (particularly SEED funding via EUR/ACE). The UN and OSCE also provided funding and resources for the missions. These varied organizational structures with separate funding sources created a diverse set of views and different prioritizations of missions. These entities also had a varied set of expectations regarding possible mission outcomes in Kosovo.

At the outset, the international community developed four pillars or sets of priorities that were divided between the participating entities. Essentially, this meant that the the UN's direct responsibilities (in addition to coordination of all the pillars) included administering the region, preparing it for self-government, and providing interim law enforcement. The OSCE took on institution building and democratization, which included developing the KPS, and the EU was allocated economic development. Meanwhile, this entire structure was parallel to the KFOR, which was in charge of providing security in close coordination with the UNMIK. This complex set of tasks called for close cooperation and coordination, but this often fell short due to the structural differences and the lack of consensus on uniform coordination mechanisms between the entities.

The UNMIK's mandate added to the overall complexity. While the mandate for the international mission in Kosovo provided the foundation for a strategic plan that was broadly agreed on by the participating countries/organizations, as events unfolded the structure revealed some weaknesses. This was particularly clear in relation to the violence that occurred in 2004 between the Albanian and Serb populations in Kosovo. The lack of an adequate response to this crisis revealed gaps in command structures, the weakness of the multilayered organizational structures between and within the entities providing security to the region (KFOR and UNMIK). The chaos and inadequate response to the violence on the part of the KFOR and the UNMIK also revealed a lack of agreement about uniform crisis response, which should have been part of the overall international strategy. Until a protocol had been determined by the KFOR, UNPOL, and KPS—as late as 2006 through a process of trial and error—whenever these challenges were overcome, it was often due to personal relationships between individuals working within the different entities.

The KFOR and UNMIK were additionally hampered by having to set up local operating structures from scratch since very little (including databases and institutional structures) remained intact from the Yugoslavian regime. In addition, there was confusion over which legal system could be used to deal with warlords and criminal elements. Even when the UNMIK and KFOR chose to use a system to deal with these issues, the local political establishment (due to the complicity of some members of the local elite with some of the targeted elements) was reticent and required substantial international persuasion to accept it.

Despite many challenges, KFOR and UNMIK efforts (usually on local or personal initiative) to set up viable structures to assist and collaborate on operational coordination were reasonably successful. These included communication between the civilian administrators and regional police commissioners on how to deal with the transition process, and regular meetings between the UNMIK's Deputy Police Commissioner, the Deputy Country Representative (DCR) for MSU, and the UNMIK's Strategic Military Planner. The individuals involved in these attempts at communication dealt mostly with responses to lingering violence in the region. In these and other instances, personal relationships between individuals in the various agencies/entities helped overcome structural issues, bureaucratic obstacles, and the complex array of control and coordination mechanisms used by each country involved in the mission.

From the beginning it was apparent that the international community working in Kosovo required a structure that would support unity of effort. Without that, key actors relied on a set of ad hoc measures and personal relationships that had uneven results. A similar situation prevailed within the USG interagency as well. In this instance, the agencies created ad hoc structures. The U.S. Country Team held regular meetings on justice sector assistance. These meetings were discontinued but were restarted when it became apparent that they were necessary to deal with reviving the justice sector. Oversight of justice sector programs have since been handed to the Kosovo MOIA.

Each country involved in the mission set up structures according to its own assessment of needs rather than making an effort to coordinate with other countries. Intelligence gathering operations were mostly done in this manner with an uneven regimen for information sharing between countries. This situation began to change as protocols were developed with the KP to enable regular information sharing with the international police, although sharing of sensitive intelligence material is still problematic (both with the KP and with partner nations).

Having a diverse array of countries participating in the mission presents challenges even now. Of fundamental importance is the "status neutral" positions that NATO, the OSCE, the EU, and the UN (all of which continue to provide assistance to Kosovo) maintain on the issue of Kosovo's independence. This complicates the working relationships, not only between the Kosovo government and these entities (which technically still see Kosovo as a province of Serbia), but also in the development of a coherent approach to capacity building between the multinational missions and the major donors, most of which (including the U.S., Germany and the UK) have recognized Kosovo's independence.

Recommendations

1.1. Ensure the USG has specific leadership positions within the mission, which can enable and ensure overall operational integration efforts.

1.2. Enforce unity of effort in policy and doctrine both within and between organizations with a special focus on USG efforts. At the baseline, USG agencies should set up tasks based on common policy and doctrine.

1.3. Ensure that deployed USG personnel are given a comprehensive understanding of the organizations and structures they have to interact and collaborate with prior to deployment.

1.4. Understand the overlap and/or conflict between pursuing USG goals and international goals. Include relevant participation from among local leaders to ensure "buy-in," and ensure that U.S. officials while in leadership positions do not impose U.S. policies and pursue U.S. interests to the exclusion of wider considerations and goals.

1.5. Develop a single, accepted system to facilitate intelligence cooperation and responses to criminal networks.

2. Executive Authority.

The UNMIK's mandate to operate under Executive Authority exposed some of the problems of working in a multinational environment. These included delays in and divergent approaches to: achieving the build-up of a mature

UNPOL contingent; development of a unified set of applicable laws and procedures; and priorities for building Host Nation institutions and capability.

The mandate of Executive Authority (and thus the breadth of responsibilities of the multinational commitment) meant that the countries involved in providing personnel and implementing the U.N. mandate had to find acceptable, unanimous solutions to a host of issues. By its very nature, the multinational environment with its diverse regulations, organizations, structures and personnel, made this task difficult.

This challenge was reflected across several issues. The UN plan was that interim law enforcement operations would be fulfilled by the UNPOL within 3 months of the KFOR intervention. In practice, this did not occur smoothly. The delays in deploying adequate numbers of UNPOL personnel created a situation in which the KFOR, including U.S. military and other contingents, had to assume responsibility for law and order.

The debate about which legal system to use in the region—the extant Serb system or the Kosovo legal code from the period of autonomy—became a significant issue of contention. (This was resolved in the interim by the UN's adoption of the Serb system, but this raised historic ethnic issues in a way that undermined Kosovarian belief that justice would be administered in an equitable manner). An unresolved question remains about whether the United States and the rest of the international community should consider setting up and using an interim system of laws in such crisis situations when local laws are nonexistent, subject to manipulation, ineffective, or too controversial in the local environment.

The RoL system also led to many questions about the efficacy of processes and procedures. At the ground level, KFOR troops lacked uniform procedures to maintain and enforce order. These military personnel used available authorities to detain individuals who posed a threat to a safe and secure environment, but often had to release these detainees after a short duration (usually less than 72 hours) since the military was not given a clear role in the justice and corrections process. This led to a "revolving door" situation, where criminals were detained and released on a regular basis with the KFOR unable to effect an enduring solution to the problem.

An effective response to political violence and how to deal with "spoilers" was another key issue that was not adequately addressed in the Executive Authority, leaving the various national contingents to come up with their own responses. Other issues of significance that demanded enduring responses included questions about the most effective way to transition from military operations to international civilian-led and finally local multi-ethnic civilian-led operations. These concerns were closely tied to the conduct of operations that simultaneously exert Executive Authority and build local capacities to take over from the international community.

Recommendations:

2.1. Define a comprehensive RoL system at the outset of an operation, to include a process for transitions across all phases (from military-led to international civilian-led and finally to domestic civilian-led transition).

2.1.(a). An existing system could be used in the interim to respond to immediate challenges and also be retained as transitions from military to international civilian-led operations take place.

2.1.(b). Consider development of an international model code to deal with major and violent crimes while the domestic system is built up to take over from the international community.

2.2. Establish clear standards for recruiting local police, taking into account the complex multiethnic context.

2.3. Conduct a comprehensive local security sector assessment and threat assessment prior to deployment of military personnel, and have these assessments drive force organization/training changes as necessary and relevant.

2.4. Develop a combined USG interagency response to assess LE requirements and develop plans to deal with interim requirements as local capacity is revived.

2.5. Deploy a full-spectrum of capabilities in relation to LE requirements, regardless of what USG entities are deployed.

2.5.(a). Ensure the military is prepared to conduct some law enforcement tasks and that deployed international civilian police personnel are prepared for the risks in setting up robust policing.

2.6. Develop a transition plan that includes a long-term component for developing local capabilities and ensure that the HN population understands and supports any system that is implemented.

2.7. Define clear roles for the USG military and civilian entities as part of Executive Authority mandate.

3. Use of Contractors.

The USG provided a sufficient number of qualified contracted law enforcement professionals to the mission. Over-

all they performed their tasks well, but there were challenges in recruiting, securing specific expertise, and management overhead.

While using contracted LE professionals has had both benefits and challenges, currently a contractor-dependent system is the only means by which the USG deploys large numbers of police to international operations. Existing legislation (particularly under the Tenth Amendment to the Constitution) limits USG ability to deputize state or local employees to federal roles; so these individuals can only work as advisors, contractors, or be added to the permanent federal work force. In addition, while the DoS can develop relationships with local/state LE to recruit LE personnel for overseas deployment, often local/state police stations cannot easily release their personnel and will not agree to do so absent some form of legal mandate (e.g., for National Guard and Reserve military forces). Finally, some relevant skills required in overseas contingencies are not commonly available in state and local LE forces.

For the DoS, one of the primary benefits of maintaining a contracting system means that it does not have to permanently employ more people. Contracting allows the DoS to avoid permanently hiring personnel who may only be required for a few years and also reduces the management overhead to vendors who oversee payroll, benefits, and other issues. The DoS is limited to ensuring the contracts are legal and current and to providing some oversight to the overall operation.

While not a prevalent problem, one of the related challenges of using contractors includes discipline and accountability. In some cases, companies providing contractors are reluctant to take disciplinary action against their contractors even in the face of clear violations because they want to maintain the mandated number of personnel in country. Contracts often do not specify the steps to be taken in such cases, making it difficult to take adequate disciplinary measures against offenders. This can foster a dangerous kind of impunity under which no system exists to deal with actions that are illegal or are contrary to USG strategic priorities and guidelines.

Recommendations:

3.1. The USG should continue to investigate all options for deploying civilian LE personnel, while continuing to field contractors in the interim. This may include utilizing new structures (including the Active Response Corps) to deploy personnel as necessary.

3.2. Whatever option is adopted for deploying civilian LE personnel, it will need to include a mechanism for coordinated planning between the LE contingent and the military to integrate efforts and priorities. Consider embedding some law enforcement personnel with the military Joint Staff and Combatant Commands to ensure effective transition from military to civilian LE operations.

3.3. Set up and standardize procedures for reconciling military rules of engagement with LE requirements, especially in relation to the use of force, appropriate use of contractors in complex operational settings, and authorities.

3.4. Establish standard structures that deploy federal employees alongside contractors and ensure that the contracts support USG strategic objectives.

4. Military Role.

U.S. military forces were required to fulfill substantial law and order functions, particularly in the period before the arrival of sufficient UN Police, and continued to share responsibilities since then. Although effective, lack of a consistent shared approach to law enforcement and detention, informal liaison protocols, and the slow and uneven UNPOL build-up created difficulties for the establishment of law and order.

The initial U.S. military response was focused on combat operations rather than on LE responsibilities, but this changed as the military focused on stabilization. Even after the arrival of the UNMIK civilian LE personnel and the establishment of the KPS, the military had to continue to share responsibilities and coordinate with these two entities at the operational level due to inadequate UN and local capacities.

These responses, which included measures to accommodate international military and police working together in areas of responsibility, had to be built up over time, despite expectations that there would be adequate UN civilian LE capabilities to take over the mission from the military. In addition, the lack of a robust civilian system and capacity, especially in relation to adequate detention facilities, forced the military to take on additional LE roles in relation to investigations, arrest and detention. In several cases, after detaining high value targets (HVTs) the military had to release them because the prisons and courts were unable to deal with prosecutions.

The lack of any doctrine on collaboration between the MSUs and SPUs added to the complications in coordination between LE and the military. There was no joint training or exercises to set up and reinforce coordination. Operational decisions were often driven by national agendas rather than a uniform international agenda. Different countries managed different sectors within the region and took different approaches to law enforcement. These differences became especially apparent in relation to military coordination since all operations involving more than one national contingent had to be conducted with consideration of various restrictive national caveats and involved a lengthy process of consultation and agreement on individual measures, which undermined the ability to respond quickly to crises.

However, the U.S. military was able to assist the UNMIK and local police. Though not governed by clear procedures, such support was important for boosting law enforcement capabilities at the local level, including through the conduct of joint patrols and other operational support. This cooperation differed by sector, depending on which country was in charge of the specific KFOR sector.

Recommendations:

4.1. Establish protocols for utilizing capabilities within the DoD with respect to maintenance of law and order during the transition from military to civilian authority to fill any gap prior to the arrival of international police forces.

4.2. Consider the development of an exportable stopgap RoL system. This would be an internationally accepted set of capabilities that could take into account the specific mandate and situation and allow military forces to deal with major acts of violence and serious crime in conflict contexts.

4.2.(a). The USG response to the RoL needs to include a system (which could potentially be a deployable capability with a "fly away" prison and court system) that could be located either within the DoS, DoJ, or DoD, and provide one of these agencies with the ability to address crime and related issues that are often present in transition settings.

4.2(b). An exportable/"fly away" RoL system needs to include clear communication with the local population to ensure that they understand that the system is not a military court, but an interim measure that will be discontinued once the local RoL system is able to deal with cases.

4.2.(c). These courts must be structured to deal mainly with serious crime and not all manner of petty crime. This would involve an expansion of the military's current ability to detain (but not arrest) people. In conceiving and implementing this system, it is important to ensure that the local RoL system is able to take charge of detainees and prosecute them as relevant.

5. Organized Crime.

Organized crime continues to be a potentially destabilizing element and has added to the complexity of the environment. It also exacerbates complications in coordination between international, multinational, and domestic groups.

Organized crime is a growing concern for the region and continues to impact Kosovo and other neighboring countries in diverse ways. The nexus between organized crime and politics is also of concern to the international community. Due to the impact organized crime has in the wider region and into western Europe, some countries are more concerned with tackling organized crime rapidly while other members of the international community take a longer view. Italy, for example, is concerned with the vast amount of contraband that enters its territory through organized criminal gangs, including from Kosovo and other countries in the region.

For the international community this involves a series of choices about whether and what action should be taken to deal with crime and the complexity of the region. For example, there is little agreement on whether the bulk of the efforts should be focused on serious crime rather than petty crime, which is also prolific, and impacts the everyday lives of Kosovars and their confidence in their government. These needs have also to be balanced against local concerns about the imposition of foreign value systems on the domestic system.

Recommendations:

5.1. Set up a system to analyze and address the relationship between organized crime and political power, which may have an impact on national stability or have the potential to create/drive conflict.

5.2. Increase HN law enforcement organizations' ability to deal with organized crime, including through the creation of domestic crime task forces and related measures.

5.3. Develop clear programs and resources to help local police deal with petty crimes to prevent the perception of impunity.

5.4. Enable HN capability to address organized crime independently, but with ongoing support from the international community.

6. Border Security.

The complexity and importance of border security demanded comprehensive multiple responses across a series of agencies. This was not adequately recognized in pre-deployment military planning and insufficient control over elements of the border continues to create problems for the Kosovo Government.

The Kosovo government continues to face shortcomings in facilities and adequate infrastructure to deal with border controls and security. This gap in the government's ability to monitor and control its borders is further complicated by the fact that Kosovo is landlocked and shares international boundaries with four countries.[16] The lack of effective border controls aids the growth and impunity of organized criminals who use these borders to traffic in contraband and people. In addition, the movement and return of displaced people creates a host of issues relating to border recognition and citizenship; all of this undermines effective governance. The UNMIK and the rest of the international community involved in the Kosovo Mission have responded to the issue and succeeded in building some capacity among Kosovo government entities.

The issue of border controls and security extends as far back as 2001 when NATO attempted to seal the border with Macedonia, which showed signs of sliding into violence, but the international military personnel involved in the effort quickly realized there was not enough manpower to respond to this demand effectively. While direct border controls remain insufficient in Kosovo, sections of the border where controls have improved with international help have led to other problems, including criminals using other means (including traditional transportation methods) to transport contraband through unofficial crossings and forcing their way through checkpoints using the threat of force. These challenges have required the international military to support and often manage checkpoints and provide additional surveillance and controls. In addition, the existing border checkpoints remain under capacity and unable to check vehicles and passengers adequately due to shortages in technology and trained customs inspection personnel.

Despite the many challenges, coordination is working well between USG agencies involved in providing assistance, training or capacity building to the HN personnel. However, more improvements are required including the sequencing of training so that capacities are built to serve the border requirements in the long term while also ensuring that the required agencies and expert personnel are brought in as part of a long-term solution.

Recommendations:

6.1. Deal with the issue of border security and controls in terms of long-term efficacy while considering its impact on internal stability. This includes setting up applicable laws, customs and tariff measures (to increase revenue collection), counter-trafficking, and systems to deal with displaced persons crossing borders.

6.2. Ensure that applicable laws associated with border security (e.g., taxes/tariffs on petroleum or cigarettes, immigration procedures, and organic laws for border security forces) are considered and addressed comprehensively.

6.3. Consider using U.S. Customs and Border Patrol expertise to assist border management forces.

This includes building in and providing the relevant skill sets, capacities, and technology, and introducing relevant international expertise.

6.4. Leverage available technology (sensors, scanners and unmanned aerial vehicles [UAVs]), and especially affordable and sustainable technology that can be left behind and supported once the international community leaves.

6.4.(a). Deploy new technologies in a deliberate manner. This should be sequenced so that HN personnel will have the capability and willingness to use and maintain them.

6.5. Develop a framework for transition of border-related tasks to HN agencies. The framework should be based on a consensus within the UN and the nations involved in supporting border operations.

6.6. Use the military to secure border crossing points only as an interim and when no other alternatives are available. The military, however, has advantages in deploying cross-country, maritime/riverine, and aerial mobility and technical surveillance platforms which are of invaluable assistance to border patrolling and thus can continue to support and provide operational assistance to international and/or HN civilian LE agencies working on border security.

6.7. Develop regional funding mechanisms to support both sides of a given border. This can help ensure that border security is a shared responsibility and valuable to populations on both sides.

6.8. Use border security and management as an intelligence gathering opportunity. This includes placing international experts with HN personnel to ensure accurate and effective information, data gathering and sharing.

CONCLUSION

Despite LE issues not being a major reason for the USG's involvement in Kosovo, LE and related aspects of the operation have together been an important part of the U.S. commitment and will continue to be. It is also a reflection of the prominence that the three interrelated strands seen here (interim international enforcement of law, host nation LE capacity building, and support to law enforcement by military forces) are likely to have in other post-conflict intervention missions. The protracted length, the magnitude, and the various levels of complexity of the U.S. law enforcement commitment to Kosovo are worth noting.

The USG has maintained a substantial and unbroken commitment in Kosovo for more than 10 years. Although the size of the overall commitment has drawn down over the course of that time, the United States still remains the largest single contributor, and there are few indications of when all elements of the commitment will be withdrawn completely. This length of commitment is significant given that the United States has had two changes of administration and has seen a dramatic change in its global security circumstances and priorities in the intervening period. Internationally, the period has also seen fluctuations in the levels of support to and interest in Kosovo by the main partner nations involved, and the decline of UN and OSCE involvement there has changed the nature of the mission markedly. Despite these factors, the United States has kept a consistent policy line toward support for Kosovo.

The magnitude of the operation in Kosovo is reflected in all three aspects of the LE commitment there. The commitment of a reinforced brigade (most of which remained in Kosovo as of 2009) as a component of a NATO force consisting of a further four brigades (numbering 50,000 at its peak) was, by the standards of the late 1990s, a large military commitment (of course, it has been dwarfed by the size of the U.S. military commitments in Iraq and Afghanistan) and the remaining force is still large, considering that Kosovo is a nation of less than two million inhabitants. The establishment of the KP and the rehabilitation/establishment of the necessary bureaucracy and rule of law infrastructure was a substantial undertaking in its own right and occurred while simultaneously maintaining security with the international military and police presence.

The complexity of the involvement in Kosovo occurred on several levels and created technical, coordination, and diplomatic demands for the USG agencies involved. Beyond the complexity of the tasks undertaken within Kosovo, the range of USG agencies involved, including bureaus and agencies related to three major government departments, required the establishment of temporary working groups among these agencies to coordinate the necessary cooperation, liaison, and funding mechanisms in order to ensure the appropriate breadth of expertise and capabilities could be provided. Given the high profile of the Kosovo operation at its inception and the recent experiences in cooperating on Haiti and similar operations, this was relatively successful at the highest level. However, the detailed military and civilian planning were conducted by different channels. Internationally, even though the United States was a major contributor to operations in Kosovo and was prominent in the diplomacy that led up to the intervention, the USG was willing to work through multinational organizations (NATO, UN, OSCE, and EU) for most of its involvement and worked under foreign leadership in each of the missions. This meant that on the ground in Kosovo, the development of formal arrangements for cooperation between the various LOOs was left in the control of the multinational missions. In practice, the coordination and cooperation necessary to deal with this complexity occurred due to local arrangements and relationships. Although solutions were found, this creates the potential for inconsistencies in approach across the theater and leaves cooperation at the mercy of personal relationships. Working with international partners also required dealing with different long-term objectives (the issue of Kosovo's independence is the most marked example), and the effect of national caveats on the conduct of operations, as well as problems with the sharing of intelligence material and developing an HN capability assisted by partner nations with different approaches to and procedures for the conduct of LE. These are all issues that will need to be addressed in any future multinational mission.

Kosovo is an interesting case study of USG involvement in LE as a component of a wider international commitment. The USG may not again face the same specific set of circumstances involved in Kosovo on future operations. However, the range of observations that can be drawn from a commitment that was so comprehensive in what it sought to achieve and involved such a number of interagency and international actors should be useful in decisionmaking and planning for other theaters and for capability development.

See Table 4-2 for summary of Kosovo observations and recommendations.

	Observations	Recommendations
1) Control and Coordination	Numerous USG agencies were involved in interdependent parts of the mission, with disparate funding lines and strategic oversight. In-country coordination and planning between the USG and international partners often relied on informal and ad-hoc personal relationships and mutual willingness to cooperate.	1.1 Ensure the USG has specific leadership positions within the mission, which can enable and ensure overall operational integration efforts. 1.2 Enforce unity of effort in policy and doctrine both within and between organizations with a special focus on USG efforts. At the baseline, USG agencies should set up tasks based on common policy and doctrine. 1.3 Ensure that deployed USG personnel are given a comprehensive understanding of the organizations and structures they have to interact and collaborate with prior to deployment. 1.4 Understand the overlap and/or conflict between pursuing USG goals and international goals. Include relevant participation from among local leaders to ensure "buy-in," and ensure that U.S. officials, while in leadership positions, do not impose U.S. policies and pursue U.S. interests to the exclusion of wider considerations and goals. 1.5 Develop a single, accepted system to facilitate intelligence cooperation and responses to criminal networks.
2) Executive Authority	The UNMIK's mandate to operate under Executive Authority exposed some of the problems of working in a multinational environment. These included delays in and divergent approaches to: achieving the build-up of a mature UNPOL contingent; development of a unified set of applicable laws and procedures; and priorities for building HN institutions and capability.	2.1 Define a comprehensive RoL system at the outset of an operation, to include a process for transitions across all phases (from military-led to international civilian-led and finally to domestic civilian-led transition). 2.1(a) An existing system could be used in the interim to respond to immediate challenges and also be retained as transitions from military to international civilian-led operations take place. 2.1(b) Consider development of an international model code to deal with major and violent crimes while the domestic system is built up to take over from the international community. 2.2 Establish clear standards for recruiting local police, taking into account the complex multi-ethnic context. 2.3 Conduct a comprehensive local security sector assessment and threat assessment prior to deployment of military personnel, and have these assessments drive force organization/training changes as necessary and relevant. 2.4 Develop combined USG interagency response to assess law enforcement requirements and develop plans to deal with interim requirements as local capacity is revived. 2.5 Deploy a full-spectrum of capabilities in relation to law enforcement requirements, regardless of what USG entities are deployed. 2.5(a) Ensure the military is prepared to conduct some law enforcement tasks and that deployed international civilian police personnel are prepared for the risks in setting up robust policing. 2.6 Develop a transition plan that includes a long-term component for developing local capabilities and ensure that the HN population understands and supports any system that is implemented. 2.7 Define clear roles for the USG military and civilian entities as part of the Executive Authority mandate.

Table 4-2. Summary of Observations and Recommendations from Kosovo.

3) Use of Contractors	The USG provided a sufficient number of qualified contracted law enforcement professionals to the mission. Overall they performed their tasks well, but there were challenges in recruiting, securing specific expertise, and management overhead.	3.1 The USG should continue to investigate all options for deploying civilian law enforcement personnel while continuing to field contractors in the interim. This may include utilizing new structures (including the Active Response Corps) to deploy personnel as necessary. 3.2 Whatever option is adopted for deploying civilian law enforcement personnel, it will need to include a mechanism for coordinated planning between the law enforcement contingent and the military to integrate efforts and priorities. Consider embedding some law enforcement personnel with the military Joint Staff and Combatant Commands to ensure effective transition from military to civilian law enforcement operations. 3.3 Set up and standardize procedures for reconciling military rules of engagement with law enforcement requirements, especially in relation to the use of force, appropriate use of contractors in complex operational settings, and authorities. 3.4 Establish standard structures (such as the model used by ICITAP) that deploy federal employees to manage contractors and ensure that the contracts support USG strategic objectives.
4) Military Role	US military forces were required to fulfill substantial law and order functions, particularly in the period before the arrival of sufficient UN Police, but continued to share responsibilities since then. Although effective, lack of a consistent, shared approach to law enforcement and detention, informal liaison protocols, and the slow and uneven UNPOL build-up created difficulties for the establishment of RoL.	4.1 Establish protocols for utilizing capabilities within the DoD with respect to maintenance of law and order during the transition from military to civilian authority to fill any gap prior to the arrival of international police forces. 4.2 Consider the development of an exportable stopgap RoL system. This would be an internationally accepted set of capabilities that could take into account the specific mandate and situation and allow military forces to deal with major acts of violence and serious crime in conflict contexts. 4.2(a) The USG response to the RoL needs to include a system, that could potentially be a deployable capability with a "fly away" prison and court system that could be located either within the DoS, DoJ, or DoD and provide one of these agencies with the ability to address crime and related issues that are often present in transition settings. 4.2(b) An exportable/fly away RoL system needs to include clear communication with the local population to ensure that they understand that the system it is not a military court, but an interim measure that will be discontinued once the local RoL system is able to deal with cases. 4.2(c) These courts must be structured to deal mainly with serious crime and not all manner of petty crime. This would involve an expansion of the military's current ability to detain (but not arrest) people. In conceiving and implementing this system, it is important to ensure that the local RoL system is able to take charge of detainees and prosecute them as relevant.

Table 4-2. Summary of Observations and Recommendations from Kosovo. (cont.)

5) Organized Crime	Organized crime continues to be a potentially de-stabilizing element and has added to the complexity of the environment. It also exacerbates complications in coordination between international, multinational and domestic groups.	5.1 Set up a system to analyze and address the relationship between organized crime and political power, which may have an impact on national stability or have the potential to create/drive conflict. 5.2 Increase HN law enforcement organizations' ability to deal with organized crime, including through the creation of domestic crime task forces and related measures. 5.3 Develop clear programs and resources to help local police deal with petty crimes to prevent the perception of impunity. 5.4 Enable host nation capability to address organized crime independently but with ongoing support from the international community.
6) Border Security	The complexity and importance of border security demanded comprehensive multiple responses across a series of agencies. This was not adequately recognized in predeployment military planning and insufficient control over elements of the border continues to create problems for the Kosovo Government.	6.1 Deal with the issue of border security and controls in terms of long-term efficacy while considering its impact on internal stability. This includes setting up applicable laws, customs and tariff measures (to increase revenue collection), counter-trafficking, and systems to deal with displaced persons crossing borders. 6.2 Ensure that applicable laws associated with border security (e.g., taxes/tariffs on petroleum or cigarettes, immigration procedures and organic laws for border security forces) are considered and addressed comprehensively. 6.3 Consider using U.S. Customs and Border Patrol expertise to assist border management forces. This includes building in and providing the relevant skill sets, capacities, and technology, and introducing relevant international expertise. 6.4. Leverage available technology (sensors, scanners and UAVs), and especially affordable and sustainable technology that can be left behind and supported once the international community leaves. 6.4.(a) Deploy new technologies in a deliberate manner. This should be sequenced so that HN personnel will have the capability and willingness to use and maintain them. 6.5 Develop a framework for transition of border-related tasks to HN agencies. The framework should be based on a consensus with the UN and the nations involved in supporting border operations. 6.6 Use the military to secure the border crossing points only as an interim and when no other alternatives are available. The military, however, has advantages in deploying cross-country, maritime/riverine and aerial mobility and technical surveillance platforms which are of invaluable assistance to border patrolling and thus can continue to support and provide operational assistance to international and/or HN civilian law enforcement agencies working on border security. 6.7 Develop regional funding mechanisms to support both sides of a given border. This can help ensure that border security is a shared responsibility and valuable to populations on both sides. 6.8 Use border security and management as an intelligence gathering opportunity. This includes placing international experts with HN personnel to ensure accurate and effective information, data gathering and sharing.

Table 4-2. Summary of Observations and Recommendations from Kosovo. (cont.)

ENDNOTES - CHAPTER 4

1. In all cases the contractors were under more direct supervision from active duty police or federal employees, rather than other contractors.

2. This is not to suggest that the USG involvement was planned in this way or even that the USG now manages its involvement in Kosovo in terms of LOOs. Rather, the LOOs are presented here purely as a (*post facto*) means to understand the continuity and breadth of ways in which law enforcement contributed to achievement of USG objectives in Kosovo.

3. United Nations Interim Administration Mission in Kosovo, *UNMIK – Fact Sheet*, June 2008, available from *www.unmikonline.org/docs/2008/Fact_Sheet_July_2008.pdf*.

4. Halvor A. Hartz and Laura Mercean, "Safeguarding a Viable Peace: Institutionalizing the Rule of Law," in Jock Covey, Michael J. Dziedzic and Leonard R. Hawley, eds., *The Quest for a Viable Peace: International Intervention and Strategies for Conflict Transformation*, Washington, DC: United States Institute of Peace, 2005.

5. Each SPU was a unit of UN police provided by a single nation which was organized, tasked, and equipped to operate as a formed body, primarily in crowd/riot control tasks (but also used for protective operations). The UN now refers to these types of units as Formed Police Units (FPUs), and FPUs now make up a substantial proportion of the UNPOL strength in most major UN operations.

6. In contrast to SPUs, MSUs were under military (KFOR) command and were formed bodies of personnel drawn from European *Gendarmerie* and *Carabinieri* forces (i.e., military personnel/units that are employed in a comprehensive LE role in their home nations).

7. Robert M. Perito, "Odd Jobs: Constabulary Forces in Kosovo," in Robert M. Perito, ed., *Where is the Lone Ranger When We Need Him: America's Search for a Postconflict Stability Force*, Washington, DC: United States Institute of Peace, 2004.

8. Hartz and Mercean.

9. United Nations Security Council Resolution (UNSCR) 1244, June 10, 1999, available from *www.unhcr.org/refworld/docid/3b00F27216.html*. As long as UNSCR 1244 remains in effect, the UNMIK retains a staff of some 50 personnel in Kosovo. These are mainly support staff for the SRSG, but also includes 8-10 international police (no Americans) in protective security roles.

10. "Europe and Eurasia," ICITAP, Department of Justice, available from *www.justice.gov/criminal/icitap/programs/europe/eurasia.html*.

11. Vushtrri (known as Vucitrn in Serbian) is located approximately 16 miles north of Pristina.

12. TF (Task Force) 793 was a battalion sized MP task force based on the headquarters of 793rd MP Battalion. Subsequent MP TFs retained this naming convention; for example, TF 793 was relieved by TF 709 (based on the 709th MP Battalion).

13. UNSCR 1244.

14. Perito.

15. UNSCR 1244.

16. Kosovo shares borders with Macedonia, Albania, Montenegro, and Serbia. The border with Serbia is known as the Administrative Boundary Line by the UN, OSCE, EU, and nations that do not recognize Kosovo's independence.

CHAPTER 5

CONCLUSION

The analysis in the previous case studies has shown the pervasive and multifaceted role that law enforcement (LE) and related elements have played in U.S. involvement in contemporary international operations. Even though the set of operations investigated is not exhaustive, the three operations selected show a range of ways and conditions in which law enforcement can impact the pursuit of operational objectives; in this way, these three operations collectively are representative of how the U.S. Government (USG) can expect LE issues to impact on other operations in the future. All of these operations (even though Colombia and Kosovo are continuing) can be considered "successful" and show that the USG, either alone or in conjunction with other nations, has the range of expertise, if not always the coordination or capacity, for these tasks and has been able to find solutions to the LE issues encountered either through deliberate interagency cooperation or by a process of trial and error by practitioners to bring the appropriate suite of capabilities and expertise to bear.

WHY ARE USG LAW ENFORCEMENT ORGANIZATIONS INVOLVED IN THESE OPERATIONS?

From these three operations, there can be seen two broad reasons for USG LE operational capabilities or expertise to become involved in international operations. The difference between these reasons impacts on the types of USG agencies that are likely to become involved in the LE aspects of an operation, what roles the agencies fulfill, and how they receive their funding to support the operation. These reasons for USG involvement are not mutually exclusive.

- **USG agencies may have interest in elements of the operational environment that directly impact law enforcement in the United States.** In some cases, domestic LE concerns may be a major consideration in the USG's decision to become involved in an international operation. In the Panama operation, the enforcement of a U.S. Federal warrant (for Manuel Noriega) was an important consideration in the decision to launch the operation. During the course of the operation, U.S. Marshals Service (USMS) personnel were also able to check detainees and airport patrons against outstanding U.S. warrants. Similarly, the commitment to support Plan Colombia was made primarily to address the flow of illicit drugs (and hence the consequent domestic law enforcement issues) into the United States. This type of operation requires not only LE expertise and capability present in theater, but also needs the authority resident in specific U.S. law enforcement agencies. Hence, these operations will require involvement of U.S. (usually Federal) LE agencies; in both Panama and Colombia, this has been in the form of direct involvement by several Federal agencies in the operational theater.
- **The USG may be required to provide/contribute to the maintenance of law and order and development of sustainable LE capability in the host nation (HN) as a component of the comprehensive responsibilities assumed by the**

international operation. In contrast to Panama and Colombia, the USG involvement in Kosovo was prompted primarily by geo-strategic and political considerations, however LE aspects became a major component of the interagency and multinational campaign design. In Panama, after U.S. forces had ousted the Noriega Government, the USG needed to both maintain order in the country and rebuild HN LE agencies. In this context, LE capability and expertise are considerations but they do not *need* to be provided by agencies and personnel that have authority to enforce U.S. law. In these cases, the LE demands have been met by a mixture of direct USG-run bilateral development programs, the deployment of USG-facilitated contractors (in both operational and instructional roles) and cooperation with multinational missions (such as relying on the United Nations Interim Administration Mission in Kosovo [UNMIK] to provide the civilian LE capability in Kosovo).

KEY FINDINGS

Despite the unique circumstances and history of each operation, there are some key findings that are common to all operations considered.

In all these operations the length of commitment of USG resources to deal with law enforcement issues has exceeded original planning estimates—often by many years. A common theme that emerged across the three operations was the long-term nature of commitment necessary, requiring roughly 10 or more years to meet each operation's objectives, which exceeded initial planning estimates. Appreciating the reality that these types of missions will last a decade or more will give future USG leaders and officials a better frame of reference for planning these operations and will set more realistic expectations for U.S. commitment. Additionally, the length of these commitments has spanned at least two U.S. presidential administrations and required numerous budget justifications to extend and modify the commitment as necessary. The relative length of the USG commitment to each operation is represented in Table 5-1.

Country	Duration	Comment
Panama	Approximately 10 years (December 20, 1989—late 1999)	Calculated from the launch of Operation JUST CAUSE (OJC) until withdrawal of the International Criminal Investigative Training Assistance Program (ICITAP).
Colombia	Almost 10 years—ongoing (Late 2000—present)	Calculated from the commencement of USG commitment to Plan Colombia. (Although it must be noted that USG operational activity in Colombia predated Plan Colombia, particularly in the Andean Counter-Drug Initiative which was in place since 1989.)
Kosovo	Over 11 years—ongoing (October 1998—present)	USG involvement Kosovo began in 1998 with a short-term commitment under the Kosovo Verification Mission to monitor compliance of the Kosovo Verification Agreement. The USG remains a major contributor to the international commitment to Kosovo.

Table 5-1. Duration of USG Commitment to Operations Investigated.

Capacity building in law enforcement has been a required and substantial element of all of these operations. In all of the operations considered, capacity building of HN LE (and related institutions), whether by design or necessity, was a key element contributing to the overall success of the mission. In Panama (the earliest of the three operations), the USG became involved in capacity building when faced with the need to rebuild Panamanian LE agencies from the ground up. A commitment to capacity building was included in the preliminary planning for Colombia and Kosovo, but involvement was marked by limitations on direct USG action. In Kosovo (where there was again a need to build agencies from scratch), the initial capacity building efforts were conducted as a part of the contribution to the multinational missions. In Colombia, capacity building was conducted in support of a functioning government. But from all cases, it is clear that capacity-building requires more than organizing, training, and equipping HN LE agencies. Two additional, related considerations are apparent:

- **Institutional Reform.** In all cases, commitment was made to institutional reform efforts that aimed to promote effective democratic policing and to address corruption, political/ethnic partiality, and abusive practices. In addition to introducing these aspects into training, these efforts have included the development of oversight mechanisms, procedures, and organizations (including working closely with relevant HN ministries); and the use of vetted HN personnel and units.
- **Reforming Other Rule of Law (RoL) Sectors.** Capacity-building of LE agencies will be insufficient if the other components of the RoL system are dysfunctional. In all three operations, inadequacies in (or absence of) the HN judicial, corrections, and legal code systems also required USG/multinational attention so they could effectively work with an increased HN LE capability. Furthermore, the effective functioning and perceived fairness of these systems sometimes also rely on programs that address underlying causes of instability, access to the justice system, and court administration.

Military forces played a key role in law enforcement and related issues, even if not specifically tasked with a law enforcement mandate. In the three operations that were analyzed in this project, it is apparent that the military has a key role to play in supporting LE priorities and objectives within an operation. Most often, military forces are first on the ground and have the greatest capability and manpower to secure and administer an area of operations. General purpose military units can also support an array of LE functions, including riot control support, patrolling of populated areas, targeting organized crime, and the provision of security to enable the conduct of LE tasks. The military also has the resources to conduct some training including skills such as patrolling, shooting, and basic investigations, and supply materiel to HN or coalition LE agencies (within the limitations of their mandate and standing USG legislation). Specialist military LE assets like military police (MPs) and the Criminal Investigation Division (CID), while primarily trained, organized, and tasked to police military operations, have an ability to fill gaps in overseas contingencies until international or HN civilian LE can take over. Given the usual disparity between military and civilian manpower, resources, capabilities, and logistics, military forces often need to retain important LE responsibilities in support of, in cooperation with, or in lieu of civilian law enforcement. The military also brings additional specialist abilities that are increasingly necessary, especially in the types of contexts into which USG personnel are being deployed. These include explosive ordnance demolition (EOD); intelligence gathering and coordination; strong kinetic backup and support for LE missions; logistics;

and strong command and control (C2) platforms and technologies. In addition, the military is able to draw upon a range of capabilities and law enforcement experience resident in National Guard and Reserve personnel. Military and LE collaboration is especially important in areas that straddle civilian LE and military responsibilities, such as border security, dealing with significant violent crime and terrorism, and in establishing and maintaining security in conflict situations. As the usual first USG (or international) presence on the ground, military forces find themselves dealing with criminal investigations in the absence of functioning court and corrections systems. The military's actions in resolving these issues will shape the environment of and lay the foundation for later efforts to build more sustainable local LE capabilities. Whom the military chooses to work with and how it builds temporary LE structures all have implications for the long-term success of the effort.

Much of the required expertise and authority for law enforcement operations and related capacity building/institutional reform exists in civilian agencies across the USG, but coordination across the USG has been ad hoc and has yielded mixed results. The key to further enhancing LE capabilities lies in bringing together military and LE skills and ensuring they are able to collaborate more effectively. LE capabilities are most important in building RoL and civil governance capabilities and capacities. The case studies highlight clearly the need for an enhanced and coordinated policy and combined planning as precursors to USG operations. While working groups often coordinate policy at the Assistant Secretary or Deputy Assistant Secretary levels, there is often inadequate coordination at levels below these where the operational-level tasks are organized and managed. When effective coordination takes place, it is often due to the personalities involved rather than due to functioning systems. Most often, military and civilian planning takes place separately and with different objectives and approaches. The military planning culture is not shared by civilian agencies, which have less formalized procedures and fewer resources. It is important to ensure the military has improved awareness of the strategic context, which is driven by civilian leadership to avoid being ahead of or out of synch with U.S. policy objectives. However, the civilian agencies in turn require enhanced abilities to provide the requisite guidance and communication to the military and must actively pursue collaboration with military planners.

IMPLICATIONS FOR THE U.S. GOVERNMENT IN LAW ENFORCEMENT ASPECTS OF INTERNATIONAL OPERATIONS

The analyses conducted in previous chapters and the key findings above highlight a number of issues related to LE roles and responsibilities that can expect to impact on the conduct of future international operations. From this can be drawn some implications for the USG to consider in its approaches to planning for international operations.

Without broader mandates and more flexible resourcing mechanisms for civilian USG LE agencies, the USG will continue to face complications in using these USG LE agencies as part of an interagency (IA) international operation. Current arrangements, under which USG agencies have funding tied to domestic law enforcement and/or specific contributions to international operations, make it difficult for the USG to fully capitalize on the capabilities and expertise already resident in these agencies and to integrate their efforts into an IA approach. Consideration should be given to determining mechanisms for permitting a more comprehensive contribution to international operations by expertise/capabilities from USG LE agencies in a manner that is not limited to supporting domestic LE priorities. Ideally, an agency's mission, tasks and resources for involvement in an international operation should be allocated in a manner that supports planning over the entire likely course of the operational involvement.

Military forces can expect that they will need to play a legitimate and substantial law enforcement role on future operations. Military forces need to accept as a legitimate part of their role that they will often be required to make a necessary and substantial contribution in aspects of LE, particularly early in an operational intervention. Despite any extant policy limiting the use of military forces in LE roles or the planned deployment of international civilian police, military forces (as the first responder and with the most substantial manpower and logistic capacities) will often be the sole security force in a theater and many of their security responsibilities and operations will approximate LE. Even after the arrival of any international or HN police capability, a military force can expect to share many security responsibilities, and to coordinate operations, with the police. Furthermore, the actions of military forces in the initial stages of a deployment can, and often will, shape the development of efforts to establish/reestablish HN law enforcement and RoL capability. Once this responsibility is accepted, it also becomes necessary to review and set up the contours of the tasks that will need to be accomplished. These will include supporting the shape and direction of the training and support to local LE. These responsibilities should be accepted as likely and legitimate for military forces and explicitly recognized in guidance and planning for international operations.

Military forces need to be prepared to be responsible for providing logistics and communications for the USG IA commitment in the initial stages of an international operation. Civilian agencies can be expected to transition their communications to their own arrangements and are likely to establish arrangements for tactical and operational-level logistics as their own operational footprint develops. However, early military-civilian planning and cooperation will facilitate the efficient build up of civilian LE expertise in theater and facilitate coordination between USG agencies in theater and in the Continental United States (CONUS).

Effective cooperation between military forces and agencies with an LE focus will be facilitated by better understanding of their respective inherent differences in cultural/organizational imperatives and perspectives. Despite overt similarities in organization (as uniformed and armed representatives of the state), military and USG LE agencies have different roles and purposes. This results in differences in perspectives and operational conduct, which can often create complications for cooperation. A common theme throughout all elements of the research was the impact of national security classifications on information sharing. This is a specific issue warranting further investigation, but it is also symptomatic of a difference in perspective between military organizations (which have a priority on maintaining both operational security and the integrity of collection assets) and LE organizations (which have a priority on maintaining the integrity of the criminal justice system; hence the need to be able to present information as evidence in an open court).

Military joint headquarters staffs should take the lead in seeking out USG civilian expertise in law enforcement resident in the USG as a routine part of their operational planning. This needs to extend beyond Department of Defense (DoD) involvement in IA working groups dealing with determining policy for LE cooperation and coordination, and into the realm of theater-level planning. This is not to suggest that the civilian role should be subordinated to military planning; rather, this will allow the IA to benefit from the military capacity for detailed planning. It will also permit the deployed military force to have better understanding of the complexities of law enforcement aspects of the operational environment and mission and plan to most effectively set the conditions for commencement of civilian programs. Specific areas for military planners to seek civilian expertise from USG LE agencies include LE capacity building/institutional reform programs; the relevant local RoL system (including LE, judicial, and corrections institutions); international civilian police (mandate, authorities, capabilities, and likely limitations); organized crime; and border management (including security, immigration, customs, and quarantine). This expertise should, where possible, be provided by representatives of USG agencies that will be responsible for each of these aspects on an operation. This will assist military planners to develop expedient solutions while ensuring a link with follow-on initiatives.

A common approach by USG agencies to the development and fielding of technologies that have relevance to law enforcement on international operations would contribute to better integration of military and civilian operations. Given the size of their budgets and their facility for supporting expeditionary operations, the DoD and military services should promote initiatives in this area. The facilitation of transition (to international civilian control and eventually to HN control) should be a consideration in military acquisition decisions for equipment or systems that contribute to the maintenance of security in an area of operations (AO); this may often mean consideration of equipment that is suitable to be left behind after the withdrawal of military forces or able to be substituted with equipment used by civilian agencies. Another consideration should be interoperability with equipment and systems used by civilian agencies; a particular area of interest is in the facilitation of military communications with nonclassified systems used by USG, international, and HN security forces.

ACRONYMS

ACI	Andean Counter-Drug Initiative
AO	area of operation
ATF	Bureau of Alcohol, Tobacco, Firearms, and Explosives
ARAVI	CNP's Air Service
AWACS	aerial warning and control systems
BACRIM	*Bandas Criminales Emergentes* (criminal gangs from Colombia)
C2	command and control
CA	civil affairs
CBP	Customs and Border Protection
CD	the Colombian Army's Counter Drug Brigade
CID	Criminal Investigation Division
CMOTF	Civil-Military Operations Task Force
CN	counternarcotics
CNP	Colombian National Police
COIN	counterinsurgency
CONUS	Continental United States
CSDI	Colombian Strategic Development Initiative
DAS	Administrative Department of Service (Colombian Security Service)
DATT	Defense Attache
DCM	Deputy Chief of Mission
DCR	Deputy Country Representative for Multinational Specialized Units (MSUs)
DEA	Drug Enforcement Administration
DIRAN	CNP's Anti-Narcotics Directorate
DoC	Department of Commerce

DoD	Department of Defense
DoJ	Department of Justice
DoS	Department of State
DoT	Department of the Treasury
DSRSG	Deputy Special Reprsentative to the UN Secretary-General
DTRA	Defense Threat Reduction Agency
ECD	Emerging Capabilities Division
EOC	emergency operations center
EOD	explosive ordnance demolition
EU	European Union
EULEX	European Union Rule of Law Mission in Kosovo
EUR/ACE	Office of the Assistance Coordinator for Europe and Eurasia (DoS)
EUR/RPM	Office of Regional Political-Military Affairs (DoS)
EUR/SCE	Office of South Central European Affairs (DoS)
EXBS	Export Control and Related Border Security (Kosovo)
EXCOMM	Executive Committee
FAA	Foreign Assistance Act of 1961
FARC	Revolutionary Armed Forces of Colombia
FBI	Federal Bureau of Investigation
GPF	general purpose forces
HN	host nation
HQ	headquarters
IA	interagency
ICE	Immigation and Customs Enforcement
ICITAP	International Criminal Investigations Training Assistance Program

ICOR	In-Country Contract Officer Representative
IDA	Institute for Defense Analyses
IDFAS	International Drug Flow Attack Strategy (of the DEA)
INL	International Narcotics and Law Enforcement Affairs (of the DoS)
INL/AAE	International Narcotics and Law Enforcement Affairs/Office of Asia, Africa, and Europe Programs
ISN	Bureau of International Security and Nonproliferation, Department of State
HVT	high value targets
JAG	Judge Advocate General
JIATF-S	Joint Interagency Task Force South
JLELT	Joint Law Enforcement Liaison Team
JLG	Judicial Liaison Group
JSRP	Justice Sector Reform Program
JTF-SOUTH	Joint Task Force South
KCPSED	Kosovo Center for Public Safety Education and Development
KFOR	Kosovo Force
KLA	Kosovo Liberation Army
KPSS	Kosovo Police Service School
KSF	Kosovo Security Force
KVM	Kosovo Verification Mission
LE	law enforcement
LECP	Law Enforcement Capabilities Project
LOO	line of operation
MilGroup	Military Group
MMA	monitoring, mentoring, and assistance

MNTF-E	Multi-National Task Force-East
MOIA	Ministery of Internal Affairs (of Kosovo)
MOS	military occupational specialty
MSU	Multinational Specialized Unit
NAS	Narcotics Affairs Section
NATO	North Atlantic Treaty Organization
NCIC	National Crime Information Center
NSC	National Security Council
NSCR	National Security Council Resolution
NSPD	National Security Policy Directive
OFAC	Office of Foreign Assets Control
OJC	Operation JUST CAUSE (Panama)
ONDCP	Office of National Drug Control Policy
OPDAT	Office of Overseas Prosecutorial Development, Assistance and Training
OPL	Operation PROMOTE LIBERTY (Panama)
OPMG	Office of the Provost Marshal General
OSCE	Organization for Security and Cooperation in Europe
OSD	Office of the Secretary of Defense
PC	Plan Colombia
PCCP	Plan Colombia Consolidation Phase
PDD	Presidential Decision Directive
PDF	Panama Defense Force
PFLD	Police Force Liaison Division (formerly USFLG)

PKSOI	Peacekeeping and Stability Operations Institute
PMO	Provost Marshal Office
PNP	Panama National Police
PTJ	Judicial Technical Police (Panama)
PSYOPS	psychological operations
RLA	resident legal advisers
RoL	rule of law
RRTO	Rapid Reaction Technology Office
S/CRS	Office of the Coordinator for Reconstruction and Stabilization (DoS)
SEED	Support for East European Democracy Act
SIU	Sensitive Investigations Unit
SME	subject matter expert
SO/LIC&IC	Special Operations/Low Intensity Conflict and Interdependent Capabilities (Office of the Secretary of Defense for Policy)
SOG	USMS Special Operations Group
SPU	Stability Police Unit
SRSG	Special Representative for the UN Secretary General
SWAT	special weapons and tactics
TAP	Technical Assistance Program
TAT	Tactical Analysis Team
U.S.	United States
UAE	United Arab Emirates
UAV	unmanned aerial vehicle
UK	United Kingdom
UN	United Nations
UNMIBH	United Nations Mission in Bosnia and Herzegovina

UNMIK	United Nations Interim Administration Mission in Kosovo
UNPOL	United Nations International Civilian Police
UNSCR	United Nations Security Council Resolution
UNTAES	United Nations Transitional Authority for Eastern Slavonia
USAF	U.S. Air Force
USAID	U.S. Agency for International Development
USARO	U.S. Army South
USFLG	U.S. Forces Liaison Group (became PFLD)
USG	U.S. Government
USMC	U.S. Marine Corps
USMC CIW	USMC Center for Irregular Warfare
USMS	U.S. Marshals Service
USSOUTHCOM	U.S. Southern Command
WHA	Western Hemisphere Affairs

ABOUT THE CONTRIBUTORS

DILSHIKA JAYAMAHA is a senior associate with Noetic. She supports Noetic's analysis of transitional law enforcement capabilities and concept development. Ms. Jayamaha has extensive experience managing programs to rebuild communities in the aftermath of conflict and natural disaster, and researching and analyzing policing in peacekeeping and stablization operations. She has run development programs in Liberia, Sri Lanka, and Colombia. With the United Nations, she ran economic revival and infrastructure projects in Sri Lanka and was an electoral officer in East Timor. Prior to that, Ms. Jayamaha worked as a journalist in Sri Lanka, India, and New York for both domestic and international agencies.

SCOTT BRADY is a senior consultant with Noetic based in Washington, DC. With Noetic, he has led two major projects looking at the employment of law enforcement on international operations. Prior to that time, Mr. Brady had served as an officer in the Australian Army for over 12 years, including two operational deployments on stabilization missions, senior staff appointments, and experience as a strategic-level analyst and an instructor of officer candidates.

BEN FITZGERALD is the country manager for Noetic's U.S. operations, having established the Washington, DC, office in November 2005. He has broad experience in strategic analysis, having worked with a wide variety of organizations in both Australia and the United States. These organizations include large federal and state government departments, defense and intelligence groups, emergency management services, and large corporations. Much of Mr. Fitzgerald's early experience was gained working for large technology organizations, helping public sector clients achieve operational outcomes through their use of technology.

JASON FRITZ is a consultant with Noetic based in Washington, DC. He has been involved in several projects providing strategic insight and analysis for various government departments and agencies. Prior to joining Noetic, Mr. Fritz served for 6 years as a cavalry officer in the U.S. Army and saw operational service on three tours of duty in Iraq. He has also provided various consulting services to the Department of State while working for other consulting firms.